When Someone You Love Drinks Too Much

When Someone You Love Drinks Too Much

A Christian Guide to Addiction, Codependence, & Recovery

Christina B. Parker

1817

A Ruth Graham Dienert Book

HARPER & ROW, PUBLISHERS, San Francisco

New York, Grand Rapids, Philadelphia, St. Louis
London, Singapore, Sydney, Tokyo, Toronto

FIRST EDITION

Library of Congress Cataloging-in-Publication Data
Parker, Christina B.
    When someone you love drinks too much: a Christian guide to addiction, codependence, and recovery/
Christina B. Parker.—1st ed.
        p.   cm.
    "A Ruth Graham Dienert book."
    ISBN 0-06-252019-9
    1. Codependence—Religious life. 2. Alcoholics—Religious life. 3. Alcoholism—Religious aspects—Christianity. 4. Codependence (Psychology)—Religious aspects—Christianity. I. Title.
BV4596.C57P37 1990
261.8'32292—dc20   89-45892
                                                            CIP

90 91 92 93 94 RRD(H) 10 9 8 7 6 5 4 3 2 1

Lovingly dedicated
to Corinna and Nora,
the jewels of my life,
and to John,
who made them
(and this book)
possible

Contents

Acknowledgments

I owe a great debt of gratitude to many. I hesitate even to mention gratitude to God in this context, for fear of trivializing a relationship so sacred I don't fully comprehend it. Yet I find He must come first on this list.

Many friends have helped and encouraged me both as a writer and in my personal growth. Although this is not a complete list, the ones that come to mind are Terry Bennett, the Caravan family—especially Ronald Caravan—Mary Dixon, Nellie Eggleton, Jeri Foster Cole, Linda Finck, Carolyn Hendrickson, Eileen Silva Kindig, Carleen Loveless, Elaine Miller, Katherine Rose, Judith Scrudato, Helen Thompson, and Janet Snow.

For giving me a good grounding in God's Word, I am deeply thankful to pastors John W. Fogal, S. Glenn Thomas, and Dennis McKenna; and also to my favorite radio teachers, Drs. Charles Swindoll and James Dobson.

Some of the first and best friends to believe in my potential were my parents, Dorothy C. and the late Robert O. Brown. They also gave me two excellent friends: my sisters Judith Brown and Janis Avery, who have been wonderfully supportive through everything.

Ray, Ann, Bill, and Ann Parker, along with Deborah and Al Carpenter, also deserve thanks for their love, kindness, and understanding.

Special thanks go to the members of my local Al-Anon and Families Victorious groups for helping to keep me honest and pointed in a constructive direction.

I am very thankful to Ruth Graham Dienert, the first editor to believe in the possibilities of this book, and to Noreen Norton and Lonnie Hull for polishing it and helping me through the publishing process with a minimum of anxiety.

Finally, I'd like to thank Harry Lorence, author of *Hay, How's Your Lawn?* Having a cousin write a book when I was young helped me to place authorship within the realm of possibility.

Introduction

Does your life revolve around a loved one who drinks too much or abuses other drugs? Mine did for many years.

In fact, my life is still deeply affected by someone else's alcoholism and probably always will be. In spite of that, God has given me more serenity and peace within myself than I ever again expected to have.

Are you suffering through sleepless nights—worrying when your loved one isn't there or enduring pointless arguments and terrible domestic disruptions when he or she is around? I've had many nights like that. If you have too, then this book is for you.

Do you feel that your life isn't your own—that you're always dancing to someone else's tune, reacting to one crisis after another rather than acting on your own goals and ideas? Do you feel trapped in a bad situation over which you have no control? So did I, but I want you to know you have more power in your situation than you think.

Do you take over responsibilities that shouldn't be yours in order to fill gaps created by your loved one's drinking or drug abuse? Have you put your own life and goals "on hold" until you can get this person straightened out? I did that too, but I found out that I had other choices.

At first, I didn't realize that alcohol was a big factor in the problems my young family was experiencing. Part of that was denial, but some part of it was also naiveté. Unlike many spouses of alcoholics, I hadn't grown up with the disease. My parents were regular, moderate social drinkers, so to me drinking was normal for adults. I hadn't much taste for it myself, but I had no idea how to recognize the destructive effects of excessive drinking. *Alcoholic* was an extreme and shocking word that had little to do with anyone I knew personally.

In my adult home, though, things were different. Finally, the domestic discord grew too terrible to be written off as "normal," and the ties to alcohol too obvious to ignore. After one horrendous night, I packed two toddlers and all their favorite toys into a station wagon and drove four hundred miles to my parents' home without telling anyone I was going. It was a "permanent" move that lasted one week—not a very mature solution.

Afterward, I began attending an Al-Anon group, because I was now convinced I needed it. I expected a heavy dose of sympathy from the group, along with some helpful bits of specific advice. Neither was forthcoming; instead, I encountered a whole new philosophy.

I quickly "bought" the Al-Anon program, read all the literature, and stored up much "head knowledge." Among the things I learned were these:

- Alcoholism is a disease.
- I didn't cause it, can't cure it, and can't control it. (That came. as a relief from a great psychological burden.)
- I too am sick, because becoming "addicted to the alcoholic" is a disease in itself.
- Though I can't change or control the drinker in my life, I can make myself happier by changing my own attitudes.
- I am responsible for my own life and happiness, and the drinker for his. The Twelve Steps of Alcoholics Anonymous (AA) and Al-Anon can help me practice a healthy responsibility.
- The attitudes I need to cultivate include acceptance of the situation, emotional detachment from the alcoholic, and recognition of the limits of my own power.
- If I allow myself to be abused, that is a symptom of my own illness.

I found that "head knowledge" wasn't enough, though. It took practice, years of it, to internalize these ideas and put them to work.

But they did help. My relationship with my husband became more peaceful and less destructive, at least for a time. The Al-Anon philosophy was not the only reason, but it was definitely a factor. There were cycles—good times and bad—but in general, I was able to live more productively by detaching myself from a problem that was not truly mine.

But I had reservations about what I heard at Al-Anon. I was also a new Christian attending an evangelical church, reading popular Christian literature, and listening to radio preachers. I was learning many sound and enduring truths, but they were put in different terms and had a different sound from the ideas taught at Al-Anon. Also, I was picking up some ideas I identified as "Christian" that caused me some doubts and conflicts:

- Real love is unconditional and does not concern itself in any way with the behavior of others.
- Having a "servant's attitude" (being like Jesus) means you allow others to treat you any way they please.
- It is "un-Christian" to take any thought for one's own rights, desires, or needs.
- Forgiveness means being willing to take the consequences of another's wrong action upon yourself.
- A wife's attitude toward her husband should be one of un-critical adoration and nearly unconditional submission. A wife must never leave her husband for any reason.

When pressed, most ministers would say that a wife is justified in separating from a husband who physically abuses her. But they don't discuss that problem unless someone else brings it up. They seem to consider it very rare.

I was confused. Were these two belief systems basically incompatible? Did the Al-Anon philosophy express a lack of Christian charity? Or were the teachings of Jesus sometimes being presented in an off-center, one-sided way?

Al-Anon principles were "working" for me. I had largely overcome my debilitating fear and self-pity, increased my self-esteem, and cut down on arguments and violence at home.

But it wasn't enough to know the program "worked." I had to know whether it squared with God's Word, on which I planned to base my life. Everything I had learned that was truly biblical also turned out to be wonderfully practical. (I believe we have a practical God.) So there was no alternative but to study the issues for myself.

Here are some things I wanted to know:

- Is it good, or bad, to set limits on the treatment I will accept from others? Does this constitute "judgment"?
- What does forgiveness really mean?
- Is it always a sin to be angry?
- Is alcoholism really a disease, or is it a sin?
- Is unconditional acceptance the highest form of love?
- Is it wrong to love myself?
- When, if ever, is marital separation a positive step?

Meanwhile, during my times of prayer, the Holy Spirit was urging me to write a book on living with alcoholism. I felt unqualified but decided to begin with research, since I still had so many unanswered questions.

I read dozens of secular and Christian books on alcoholism and related issues, took piles of notes—and became more confused. Each book gave me some useful ideas, but their overall points of view showed great diversity. None of them had a basic philosophy that made me completely comfortable. Some had good advice for the alcoholic that was useless to me without his cooperation. Some wanted me to follow a step-by-step program of specific actions, as if I were not an adult who could decide what to do once I understood the principles (and as if everyone's situation were the same.) Others advocated a "get-tough" stance without explaining where the concept of love fit in. In contrast, some books for Christian wives seemed to advise me to cultivate a soft heart and a softer brain.

Finally, I turned to the Bible, as I should have done in the first place. In my study of Proverbs, I found a wealth of relevant material to add to my notes, all of it eminently practical. Now I felt "at home." Later I found more, equally useful ideas in many other books of Scripture through studies of individual words and concepts.

This book details the answers I found and the conclusions I believe God gave me through my study of His Word and my personal experiences. It is the result of my own journey toward recovery—a journey that still continues. (At this writing, my path has led to separation from my alcoholic husband, but I don't believe the final chapter has been written on that subject.) Others might read the same Bible and draw conclusions different from mine. That's fine; I don't believe God intends us all to think exactly alike.

By now it should be clear that this book was written to myself as much as to anyone else. I do, of course, hope it will be as helpful to one who reads it as it has been to me to write it. If you are still recovering from the effects of someone else's dependence on alcohol or other drugs—or if your journey has just begun—come, take my hand. Let's walk together.

All names used in this book have been changed to protect the privacy of individuals. All incidents presented as fact are true stories—events that happened either to me or to someone I know personally.

You will note that much of my material pertains to white middle-class and working-class Americans. Much of it also deals with the situation of a male alcoholic and a female codependent rather than the reverse. This is unavoidable, given the nature of my own background and experience. I have tried to not exclude anyone in this book, but I believe much more needs to be written, especially by Christians, about chemical dependency and codependency among people of both sexes and various races, nationalities, and ethnic groups. I regret that I cannot "be all things to all people" in this way, and I challenge other Christian writers with backgrounds different from mine to begin filling the gap.

Part 1   Defining the Problem

---

1 Why Can't We Live Like Normal People?

I tried cheering myself with wine, and embracing folly—my mind still guiding me with wisdom. I wanted to see what was worthwhile for men to do under heaven during the few days of their lives. ECCLESIASTES 2:3

Evie's Story

Evie's stomach hardened into a tight knot as she heard Ted's car pull in, two hours late. It had been such a nice, peaceful week. She'd thought maybe she and Ted had turned a corner and finally left their recent problems behind them.

One look at Ted's glazed, vacant eyes told her this evening wasn't going to be a good one. When he looked at her and read the worry and disappointment in her face, his own expression turned to one of defiance, as if silently daring her to say anything about his lateness or condition. The battle lines were already drawn, and no one had spoken a word.

The children acted upset at the supper table, reacting to their parents' moods and to the long delay before eating. Joshua burst into tears when Evie said he had to finish his peas. Then Ted told him, "Shut up, or I'll give you something to cry about!"

This statement—which never in the history of the world has gotten a child to stop crying—didn't work with Joshua either. Both children ended up running off in misery to their rooms.

"This is the toughest, driest roast I've ever seen," Ted complained. "I work all day to put food on this table, and you can't do any better than this?"

"It looked plenty tender enough at five-thirty," she answered.

"You can't just keep a roast hot forever, you know. Why can't you at least call when you're going to be late?"

Ted came back with an angry reply, and another rip-roaring argument was off and running. By the time it was over, Ted had dumped the remaining contents of his plate on the floor and called Evie an obscene name; Evie had been afraid he would hit her. When she attempted to leave for a while to cool off, he wouldn't let her go. First he refused to give her the car keys, and then he barred the door with his body to keep her from leaving on foot. She responded with some choice, angry comments she would never have made under other circumstances.

After Ted finally fell asleep in his chair, Evie's tears fell on the food she scraped off the floor. Later, she stared out the window at the house across the street, which always seemed so peaceful. She had never heard a raised voice from over there. "Why can't we be as happy as Barb and Mac seem to be?" she wondered. "Why can't we live like normal people?"

Then guilt and self-doubt set in. "What am I doing wrong, that my husband wants to get drunk before he comes home at night? If I were a good enough wife, wouldn't he want to come straight home?"

Although her guilt isn't appropriate, Evie has already taken the first step toward a better life, by admitting that her family has a problem. Her situation has gotten so out of hand that she can no longer tell herself things like, "This is normal. Everyone has an argument or a bad day now and then. I shouldn't expect anything different." Owning up to a serious problem is progress, even though it doesn't feel good at the time.

Our Alcohol-Saturated Society

Did Evie's domestic tale of woe ring any bells with you? Did it remind you of your own family, or that of a friend or relative, or perhaps the home in which you grew up? Alcohol abuse has touched practically everyone in our culture in one way or another.

Drinking goes back almost to the Flood in biblical times. In Genesis 9:20–27 we learn that Noah got drunk and became estranged from one of his sons because of it. (Noah may not have known what would happen, if he was in fact the inventor of wine.)

There is hardly a country in the world today that doesn't have an alcohol problem to one degree or another, but the United States is said to have the second-highest rate of alcoholism in the world. Only in France is the rate of alcoholism higher. No one knows exactly how many alcoholics we have, but estimates range between ten and fifteen million. Two-thirds of all American adults—and a majority of our teenagers as well—drink alcoholic beverages. Of these many millions of "social drinkers," one expert says that about 10 percent will become addicted, compulsive drinkers, or alcoholics.

This simply means that though alcohol abuse should never be accepted as normal, it is extremely common in our society. Ironically, this is one reason an addicted drinker can continue for a long time to excuse his or her irresponsible behavior as "normal."

The reasons the majority of people drink are easy enough to understand. Drinking is a deeply ingrained social custom, and in many circles alcohol acts as a social lubricant. To some hosts and hostesses, it's a symbol of their hospitality—something they routinely offer all guests, in the same class with food, coffee, or a place to hang one's coat.

Then there are those who like the taste of alcoholic drinks, or the status appeal of a fine wine or expensive liquor. Some people use it as a sleeping aid or a tranquilizer; alcohol's advantage here is that it is more easily available and more socially acceptable than other drugs. It does have the predictable effect of taking one's mind off one's problems for a period of time. Then there are people who use alcohol as a painkiller, for anything from a toothache to a chronic bad back.

But the high rate of addiction to alcohol turns any possible advantages into disadvantages. Its relative cheapness, easy availability, and social acceptance just make it easier for more people to become hooked. Who would knowingly, voluntarily become a slave to a drug for any of the above reasons? No one would. Instead, each drinker insists, "I'll be careful and drink wisely. I'll be among the majority of drinkers who don't become alcoholics."

There currently is no sure way to predict which drinkers will keep their habit under control and which will lose that control. "Problem" drinkers come from both sexes and all social classes, races, religions, and ethnic backgrounds. They start out with all sorts of personalities, although they tend to become a great deal alike in their behavior as the disease progresses.

Many researchers now believe that a tendency toward alcoholism can be inherited. Some are trying to find a "genetic marker" or a physical test that would determine who is likely to have a problem.

But, we already know that a child of an alcoholic is more likely to develop the condition than anyone else, even if the child is adopted and never knows the alcoholic biological parent. It's also true that some nationalities and ethnic groups have a more pronounced problem than others, probably because of cultural as well as genetic factors; drunkenness and heavy drinking are much more acceptable in some cultures than in others.

Many people fail to recognize alcoholism in friends and family members because of certain common, preconceived ideas. We tend to think of an alcoholic as an unshaven, filthy man living in the streets, sipping cheap wine from a paper bag. (Actually, only about 5 percent of alcoholics ever are reduced to living on skid row.) Or, we think of a man whose behavior is violent and unpredictable. We always think of a *man*, though, don't we? So it takes us by surprise when a *woman* friend turns out to be a closet alcoholic, drinking all day from supplies kept under the kitchen sink with the bleaches and cleansers. And we are equally surprised when a nice, decent family man with a good job turns out to be committing slow suicide by ruining his liver with excessive drinking.

A drinker can cross the line into alcohol addiction during childhood or the teen years, during retirement, or at any age in between. Some young people seem to become hooked with their first drink and never drink "normally"; others become addicted only after many years of moderate drinking.

Some longtime members of Alcoholics Anonymous say that there are no "pure alcoholics" under age twenty-five. By that they mean younger problem drinkers usually abuse other drugs as well. They may combine illegal drugs with alcohol, use them at different times, or take whatever they can get when their "drug of choice" is unavailable. In this way they only compound their legal and financial problems and increase their confusion, their erratic behavior, and their likelihood of brain damage.

Left untreated, alcoholism, sooner or later, ends in death. And it also contributes to just about every social evil there is. It seems strange, then, that drunkenness is often treated as a laughing matter by the entertainment industry. A comedian can usually get a good laugh with a drunk act, and some have built their careers on it. It seems that our society just doesn't want to see that its "harmless diversion" has severe and devastating consequences for many people.

Moreover, the consequences of alcohol abuse are not confined to the drinker. We all suffer from it—even people who never touch a drop. Anyone who lives with an abuser of alcohol is profoundly affected. That is why alcoholism is called "the family disease." But even outside the immediate family, there are others whose lives are disrupted or inconvenienced to some degree: relatives, employers, employees, co-workers, neighbors, and friends.

It is quite likely that you have been affected by someone's excessive drinking. Have you lost a loved one in an accident caused by an intoxicated driver? Has your house been broken into by kids under the influence? Have you ever been asked to cover for a colleague who was in no condition to do his job? Have you waited in vain for an electrician who never came back from lunch, or given breakfast to a neighbor child whose mother would not wake up? And all of us pay a great deal more for our car insurance than it would cost if everyone drove only when sober.

Yes, all of us have suffered one way or another from the dread disease of alcoholism, and with the psalmist we cry out, "You have shown your people desperate times; you have given us wine that makes us stagger. . . . Save us and help us with your right hand, that those you love may be delivered" (Ps. 60:3, 5).

2 *The Consequences of Alcoholism*

Who has woe? Who has sorrow? Who has strife? Who has complaints? Who has needless bruises? Who has bloodshot eyes? Those who linger over wine, who go to sample bowls of mixed wine. PROVERBS 23:29–30

Abusers of alcohol harm themselves and those around them in many ways. The brief list I offer here, which is not all-inclusive, will set forth four main categories of harm.

Physical Harm

Alcohol acts as a depressant on the central nervous system. It is a poison: a fifth of a gallon of whiskey in an hour can paralyze the brain stem, causing coma and death. The liver can process and break down about one-half ounce of pure alcohol in an hour, which is the amount contained in an average drink: one to one and a half ounces of liquor, five ounces of wine, or twelve onces of beer. When a person has more than one such drink in an hour, the rest of the alcohol circulates in the bloodstream "waiting its turn" to be broken down. So the number of drinks taken determines the approximate number of hours the drinker will be under the influence. While it's in the bloodstream, the circulating alcohol affects every organ and system of the body.

Probably the best-known physical consequence of heavy drinking is cirrhosis of the liver—a buildup of excess connective tissue caused by slow poisoning, which often leads to death. The "beer belly" so often joked about is frequently a sign of a swollen liver and the water retention that goes with it. Kidney disease of various kinds, pancreatitis, ulcers, and diabetes can all be made much worse by drinking.

Alcoholics have a greatly increased risk of getting tuberculosis, even now when we think of TB as a conquered disease. But the alcoholic has a lowered resistance to infections in general.

A person in the late stages of alcoholism often forgets to eat or is unable to keep anything down. The resulting malnutrition can cause brain damage severe enough to land the person in a nursing home, permanently. This happened to a man I knew who was barely fifty years old.

At the same time, withdrawal from alcohol is also dangerous for an addicted drinker and should be done only with medical supervision. Delirium tremens, or *d.t.*'s, can cause very realistic and frightening hallucinations; sudden withdrawal can also lead to convulsions and even death. However, for a drinker with a milder dependency, withdrawal usually results in "the shakes" and excessive perspiration.

These so-called natural causes of death are not the only way alcoholics shorten their life expectancy by an average of ten to twelve years. Accidental deaths claim many drinkers and the people around them. (Such drinkers don't have to be alcoholics, of course, but alcoholics can be expected to be under the influence more often than others.) The number of traffic deaths caused by drunken driving has hovered around twenty-five thousand annually in the United States for many years, with many thousands more injured. Fortunately, tougher enforcement of the law has begun to make a dent in this terrible statistic. For many years, our courts and legislatures didn't seem to regard intoxicated driving as a real crime, but dedicated groups of concerned citizens have been working to change their minds and to change public behavior.

But there is another important question. What about accidental deaths that do not involve highway vehicles? A great many home and industrial accidents are said to be alcohol related, and no one knows how many fires, drownings, hunting accidents, falls, electrocutions, and so on have alcohol as a contributing factor. In the city where I live, for example, a fisherman who had consumed several beers fell to his death from a stone stairway on the riverbank.

Alcohol abusers can die from their condition in more ways than we can think of. A woman I knew was drinking one cold night and wandered outside to the family swing set, where she was found in the morning dead of hypothermia. A close friend, a man in his fifties, died at home one Sunday afternoon after drinking a great deal of alcohol, passing out, and inhaling his own vomit.

Experts have estimated that 35 to 40 percent of suicides are alcohol related, and that in half of all homicides, the assailant and/or the victim has been drinking. Alcohol is also a large factor in child abuse and family violence. And, of course, no one can even guess how many days and hours are spent in unproductive misery because of hangovers.

Financial Harm

"For drunkards and gluttons become poor, and drowsiness clothes them in rags" (Prov. 23:21). Spending more than one can afford on liquor is merely the beginning of the financial consequences of alcohol abuse. These can include the loss of a job due to poor performance, or the failure of a self-owned business because of poor management. A drinker's judgment is just as likely to be impaired in financial as in other matters, but he or she doesn't realize it at the time. Heavy drinkers may miss appointments, make poor decisions, enjoy playing the "big spender" with associates, make unwise loans, or invest in foolish schemes. Drinkers who work with their hands, whether repairing computers or performing surgery, will lose judgment and coordination and make costly mistakes.

Alcoholics in business will insist that they have to spend a great deal of time in bars to make contacts. They surround themselves with others who live in the same state of mental fog, and they are oblivious to the fact that nondrinkers who see their cars always in the tavern parking lot tend to avoid doing business with them.

Abusers of alcohol are liable to have to pay for property damage caused by alcohol-related accidents of various kinds. In the later stages, they may run up preventable medical bills or become unable to get health or motor vehicle insurance. Traffic violations or bad business decisions can lead to substantial legal expenses.

Mental and Emotional Harm

The problem drinker in your life is most certainly going through terrible anguish and suffering in spite of making a valiant effort to conceal it. In various ways, the drinker tries to "pass on" that misery to you and other close associates, rather than suffer it alone.

Alcohol abuse is a vicious cycle, emotionally. First a person discovers, perhaps by accident, that a drink seems to improve his or her mood, causing an emotional lift. But unfortunately, the effect soon wears off, and another drink is needed to regain that good feeling.

Eventually, drinkers develop increased tolerance, or the need to drink a greater amount of alcohol before experiencing the "lift" that was so easily obtained at first. Tolerance enables them to hold more alcohol without appearing to be drunk. But now when the mood returns to normal, "normal" is lower than it used to be. They feel increased anxiety and guilt when sober, especially about the drinking and any bad behavior that went along with it. So they drink even more, or more often, to ward off these painful feelings. This chain of events marks the gradual beginning of addiction.

We can know for sure that a drinker has crossed the line into alcohol abuse when he or she has to drink ever-increasing amounts just to feel normal. (In the late stages of alcoholism, when there is severe physical damage, tolerance drops again, and the drinker acts "drunk" after consuming very little alcohol.) And as alcohol becomes increasingly important to drinkers, they will not admit to a drinking problem. Deep inside, they are aware that this is a way of life with no future, that they are slaves to something outside themselves, and that they are committing a slow form of suicide. They consume more and more alcohol in an effort to drown feelings of anxiety.

There is an old Chinese saying: "First the man takes a drink, then the drink takes a drink, and finally the drink takes the man."

Then, as if that unhappiness weren't enough, the drinker starts to experience blackouts—chemically induced periods of amnesia. Blackouts are not to be confused with passing out. During a blackout, the drinker will look quite normal (or normally drunk)—walking, talking, and doing things—but later won't remember any of it. A blackout can last minutes, hours, or days.

At this stage, the drinker is paying a very high emotional price for those fleeting "good times": guilt, depression, anxiety, lowered self-esteem, hostility, defensiveness, self-pity, and the sneaking suspicion that life has gotten out of control. Rather than face all this, the heavy drinker practices denial: a refusal to admit to anyone the truth about loss of control.

At this stage, too, heavy drinkers are liable to turn their anger at themselves on others—a process called projection. They often lash out at others, especially those who are closest, claiming that others' faults and failures are responsible for their drinking and poor behavior. Irrational outbursts of bad temper at the slightest sign of imperfection in a spouse or family member are commonplace. And irrespective of the drinker's own faults, imperfection in others cannot be tolerated. No matter what happens, there must be someone else to blame.

Spiritual Harm

No matter what their religious background, addicted drinkers suffer grave spiritual emptiness in addition to all their other problems.

Alcoholics who have known God's grace in the past feel keenly aware of all that they are missing in terms of communion with the Lord and true fellowship with other believers. Former Christian friends have likely backed off, not knowing how to handle their current behavior and attitudes. Hurt by this, the alcoholic condemns them as hypocrites and eventually stops going to church. Then if the pastor or someone else tries to help, the drinker often explodes with anger—a cover-up for a deep-seated inner fear.

The alcoholic who knows the Bible at all cannot doubt that drunkenness is against the will of God. And this knowledge leads to a heavy load of guilt. There is no way a person can be filled with alcohol and with the Holy Spirit at the same time, as is confirmed in

Ephesians 5:18: "Do not get drunk with wine, which leads to debauchery. Instead, be filled with the Spirit."

Debauchery, the corrupt or immoral behavior that the drinker falls into, causes even greater guilt. As drinkers struggle against the knowledge that they have violated their own system of values, and choose to bury that knowledge rather than deal with it, they slip into a carnal, double-minded spiritual state. Such people are among the unhappiest in the world, even though they may appear carefree and concerned only for their own pleasure.

Even a person who has never had a personal, saving relationship with God still knows deep inside that drunkenness and its accompanying bad behavior are wrong. This feeling may keep that person from even approaching God. For at such times the Enemy works subtly to convince the alcoholic that God can't and won't forgive anyone so low and unworthy.

As the apostle Paul said, "Christ Jesus came into the world to save sinners—of whom I am the worst. But for that very reason I was shown mercy" (1 Tim. 1:15–16). Absolutely no one is beyond God's grace.

The drinker may also be afraid that a close relationship with God would call for an end to drinking, and that is correct. Yes, such a step would be bone-breakingly hard, but no one is expected to do it without help. Jesus assures us, "What is impossible with men is possible with God" (Luke 18:27).

The person who continues to make an idol of alcohol will most certainly suffer grave spiritual consequences, perhaps for eternity. In writing to the Corinthian Christians Paul made it clear that not "thieves nor the greedy nor drunkards nor slanderers nor swindlers will inherit the kingdom of God" (1 Cor. 6:10). And centuries before that the wisdom writer gave us these wise words:

> Do not gaze at wine when it is red,
>   when it sparkles in the cup,
>   when it goes down smoothly!
> In the end it bites like a snake
>   and poisons like a viper.

Your eyes will see strange sights
   and your mind imagine confusing things.
You will be like one sleeping on the high seas,
   lying on top of the rigging.
"They hit me," you will say, "but I'm not hurt!
   They beat me, but I don't feel it!
When will I wake up
   so I can find another drink?" (Prov. 23:31–35).

3 *Sin, Disease, or What?*

Wine is a mocker and beer a brawler; whoever is led astray by them is not wise.

PROVERBS 20:1

Have you noticed that, so far, we have described alcoholism quite a bit but haven't defined it? Writing a definition of alcoholism is such a thorny task that many books on the subject never attempt it at all. We're told what to do about the condition without being told what it is. The reason for this is that when we try to define alcoholism, we run into certain controversies that may become roadblocks for you, the spouse or close associate of a problem drinker, in your quest for a better life. However, as we take a closer look at the problem, we'll see this need not be the case.

A Tricky Question

First comes the question, is alcohol abuse a disease or a sin? In response, the medical profession, Alcoholics Anonymous, and many Christians say, "Alcoholism is a disease. Nobody chooses to have it, and those who do need compassion and professional treatment."

By contrast, there are those Christians who say, "Nuts to that! Drunkenness is a sin; that's all there is to it, and we shouldn't condone or excuse it by making up this so-called disease of alcoholism!"

Now, no matter which of these two responses (if either) is acceptable to you, it is important that this question not become a stumbling block in your path toward personal growth. Your plan of action for improving the quality of your life remains the same! Your primary focus should be on your own life and how you choose to live it. If you

15

do further research into the subject you may even conclude, as I have, that drunkenness is a sin *and* alcoholism is a disease. The two ideas really are not mutually exclusive. Let's see why.

Drunkenness Is a Sin

There is no doubt that both the Old and New Testaments classify drunkenness as a sin and the drunkard as a sinner. From Noah and Lot to the later kings of Israel and Judah, drunkenness was a condition that led to incest, murder, military defeat, and other disasters (in a word, debauchery, as we saw in Ephesians 5:18).

Without question, drunkenness in ancient biblical days was seen as a sin in itself. In Deuteronomy 21:18–21, parents of a rebellious, habitually drunken son are instructed to take the boy out and have him stoned to death. (Even the threat of such a solution must have been very sobering. Let's hope that parents used this idea in motivating more than in actual practice.)

Jesus himself condemned those who get drunk and neglect their responsibilities, saying they deserve "a place with the unbelievers" (Luke 12:42–46). And drunkenness is high on the lists of sins spoken against in the writings of Paul and Peter. In writing to the Christians in Galatia, Paul said, "The acts of the sinful nature are obvious: sexual immorality, impurity and debauchery; idolatry and witchcraft; hatred, discord, jealousy, fits of rage, selfish ambition, dissensions, factions and envy; drunkenness, orgies, and the like" (Gal. 5:19–21).

In other New Testament writings such acts are called "deeds of darkness" (Rom. 13:12–13) and a "flood of dissipation" (1 Pet. 4:3–4).

It is true that many nonaddicted drinkers choose to get drunk as a recreational activity. But to make such a choice is to expose oneself to the possibility of committing every other sin on the list through lowered inhibitions. It also shows indifference to the real possiblity of accident, injury to others as well as oneself, and future addiction. To make such a choice is to consciously thumb one's nose at God and the world and say, "I don't care."

But then comes the question, Is the addicted drinker capable of making this choice, or is it out of his or her hands? Certainly the alcoholic's capacity for free choice is reduced. My own opinion, though, is that alcoholics usually know deep down, that they are out of control. Generally, addicts also know that treatment is available. If a person chooses not to take the treatment, that is also a choice. Drunkenness is still a sin.

Alcoholism Is a Disease

The Bible presents drunkenness as a deliberate act of disobedience. By contrast, medical definitions of alcoholism revolve around loss of control on the part of the drinker.

This definition comes to us by way of the American Medical Association: "Alcoholism is an illness characterized by preoccupation with alcohol; by loss of control over its consumption, such as usually leads to intoxication or drinking done by chronicity; by progression and by tendency to relapse. It is typically associated with physical disability and impaired emotional, occupational, and/or social adjustments as a direct consequence of persistent and effective use."

"Loss of control" means that alcoholics cannot predict with any reliability whether a particular drinking episode will be "normal," that is, whether they will be able to stop when they choose, or "abnormal," resulting in drunkenness in spite of their best intentions.

For example, let's say that on Monday Donna decides to have two drinks with her co-workers on the way home. She does just that and arrives home in time to fix a good supper. No problem. Then on Wednesday she decides to do the same thing. But suddenly, hours later, she is drunk and honestly doesn't know how it happened. Donna is an alcoholic.

"Progression" means that without treatment, the condition gets worse until the patient dies. It never improves or goes away on its own. In AA, one hears stories of alcoholics who went back to drinking after being dry for more than twenty years and found themselves "right back where they left off"—their symptoms as severe as ever. In no way were they "starting fresh," as if they had never had a drink before.

This is why an alcoholic can never become a "normal" social drinker, in spite of extensive treatment or a well-adjusted emotional life. Several years ago, some researchers claimed that their therapy had helped some "former alcoholics" become able to drink responsibly and moderately. Later investigation showed that their data were flawed, and that most of their patients had relapsed into active alcoholism.

Members of Alcoholics Anonymous recognize the progressive, incurable nature of their condition by referring to themselves as "recovering alcoholics," never "former alcoholics." Some recovering Christians choose not to call themselves alcoholics any longer, because they are "new creatures in Christ." They, like the AA members, have no intention of becoming social drinkers.

Progression occurs in certain recognizable stages. According to one expert, the first of three stages is marked by drinking for emotional relief and by the first incidents of drunken driving and blackouts. The second, or crucial, stage is marked by poor work performance, absenteeism, and financial and family problems. Medically, it may also include sexual impotence and liver disease. In the last stage, the sufferer probably has permanent liver and brain damage and may even have lost home and family.

Without treatment, alcoholism is fatal. If appropriate treatment begins in the crucial stage, the recovery rate may be as high as 80 percent. Even at the latest stage, as many as 25 to 30 percent of alcoholics can recover, according to some experts, enough to become employable and live a normal life.

It is possible that the majority of alcoholics also abuse sedatives and tranquilizers, which they often get by prescription. They have no more control over these than over alcohol, and will often substitute one drug for the other. This is called "cross-addiction." In such cases recovery cannot begin until they give up all such mood-altering drugs, according to knowledgeable doctors. Moreover, it is dangerous to combine pills and alcohol because each can multiply the effects of the other, and an accidentally fatal overdose has often been the result.

Born to Be Drunk?

Genetic predisposition is a concept that helps us understand why alcoholism is progressive and incurable. It has been discovered fairly recently by the researcher Virginia Davis in Houston that alcoholics actually process alcohol differently in their bodies than do nonalcoholics. For example, when the alcoholic is drinking there is a significant buildup in the brain area of a highly addictive chemical called THIQ (tetrahydroisoquinoline). However, the nonalcoholic is able to break down this chemical and dispose of it.

Apparently this chemical causes a craving for alcohol. When it is injected into the brains of laboratory rats that would normally be repulsed by alcohol, it actually makes them prefer vodka to plain water.

Furthermore, studies on monkeys have shown that THIQ stays in the brain for life once it is there. No wonder an alcoholic can stay dry for decades but still be incapable of so-called normal social drinking.

THIQ could account for the tendency of alcoholism to run in families, which is well documented. A Swedish study of adopted sons placed at birth in nonalcoholic homes showed that sons whose natural fathers were alcoholics were nine times more likely to become alcoholics than sons whose natural fathers were not alcoholics.

It seems likely that some children inherit a genetic predisposition to build up THIQ—more addictive than morphine—in their brains when and if they drink. This does not mean they are alcoholics from birth. They still have to drink to develop the condition. But if they ever start drinking, they run a high risk of addiction simply because their body chemistry is different from that of a person who can drink moderately and keep it under control.

So far, there is no test to determine whether a person carries this genetic factor. Obviously, anyone with an alcoholic parent or grandparent should be very cautious, and it would be safer not to drink at all.

However, even in the absence of a genetic predisposition, a drinker can become addicted after drinking heavily over a number of years.

Even a level of drinking that most would call moderate can be dangerous: "A person who drinks two to three drinks three or more times a
week is setting him- or herself up for trouble" in an average of seven
to ten years, according to Dr. Anderson Spickard, Jr., a professor of
medicine at Vanderbilt University Medical Center.

Other research has suggested that allergies or blood sugar problems may also play a role in alcoholism. But to date the evidence is
inconclusive. In most instances men and boys have been the subjects
of the studies that have been done. Because recent investigation
suggests there may be as many female as male alcoholics, it is important to find out whether the process works differently in women.

God's Word on Sin and Disease

As Christians, we need to examine all the important questions in
life in a scriptural light. A careful reading of the Bible shows us that
the dividing line between sin and disease can be rather fuzzy to our
limited human sight. Let's look first at three of Jesus' many miracles
of healing.

In Mark 2:2–12 we learn of a paralyzed man whom Jesus enables to
get up and walk. The Lord's first words to the man were, "Son, your
sins are forgiven." When criticized for assuming the authority to
forgive sins, Jesus replied, "Which is easier: to say to the paralytic,
'Your sins are forgiven,' or to say, 'Get up, take your mat, and
walk?'"

Of course, Jesus cured the man of both his sin and his disability,
but we can certainly conclude that the two were related, at least in
that case. The Lord again combined the two ideas in his later metaphor, "It is not the healthy who need a doctor, but the sick. I have not
come to call the righteous, but sinners" (Mark 2:17). This story and
comment can be found in three of the four Gospels.

Turning next to John 5:1–14, we have the story of Jesus healing
another paralyzed man—this time at the pool of Bethsaida. After the
man was healed, the Gospel writer says, "Later Jesus found him at
the temple and said to him, 'See, you are well again. Stop sinning or
something worse may happen to you.'"

It is also worth noting that Jesus had previously asked this man, "Do you want to get well?" as if he had some doubt about the man's motives. Perhaps there had been some "rewards" for him in becoming or remaining a long-term invalid. In each case, though, we see that Jesus never rebuked or condemned the sick and disabled; he treated them with great compassion.

However, before we start thinking that all infirmity is somehow related to sin, let's turn to the story of the blind man in the Gospel of John to whom Jesus gave both his sight and some remarkable spiritual insight: "His disciples asked him, 'Rabbi, who sinned, this man or his parents, that he was born blind?' 'Neither this man nor his parents sinned,' said Jesus, 'but this happened so that the work of God might be displayed in his life' " (John 9:2–3).

The Old Testament also shows us that sin and disease are connected in some cases, and not in others. In Psalm 38, David clearly blames his failing health on God's anger against him because of his sin. Yet in the case of Job, who was covered with painful boils from head to foot, we are told directly that no sin of his was responsible; rather, Satan was being allowed to afflict and test him to prove his faith (Job 2:1–8).

Sorting It Out

So, if sin and disease are related in some cases and if calling alcoholism a disease does not rule out the concept of sin, are we justified in referring to it as a disease? I think we are. Alcoholism affects the whole person: body, mind, emotions, and spirit. The physical component of the disease does not in any way absolve the alcoholic of moral responsibility for his or her choices, though. It isn't a case of, "Oh, the poor guy, he has a disease; he can't help anything he does."

With our emerging knowledge of the genetic factors in alcoholism, we must give up the traditional idea that the condition is caused by a weakness of character. When two new drinkers each pick up their first beer, they are morally just alike. Neither is violating a clear command of God, since nowhere does the Bible condemn all drinking of alcohol—only drunkenness is forbidden.

Suppose, though, that one of these new drinkers has a genetic predisposition to build up THIQ and the other does not. Neither one knows or believes that he or she is in danger of addiction. But one of them becomes an alcoholic even though he does not "bring it on himself deliberately." The loss of control is gradual, inconsistent, unpredictable, confusing, and clouded by denial. The alcoholic makes the same early choices as the social drinker, but with far different results.

The budding alcoholic, however, can choose to stop drinking at any time—not after having a drink or two, because loss of control occurs then—but by not picking up a drink in the first place. And if that budding alcoholic is unable to choose abstinence on his own, there is help available from God and from other supportive human beings. He generally knows this, and he also senses that he is in trouble as he gets increasing negative feedback from others and from his own feelings of guilt. Confusion and denial, as powerful as they are, are not excuses for falling deeper into trouble.

Alcoholics Anonymous has helped more alcoholics get well than any other agency on earth, and they recognize alcoholism as a disease. At the same time, though, they hold their members to a very high standard of moral responsibility for their own recovery, apparently seeing no conflict between that and the disease concept. Though not specifically Christian, its Twelve Step program emphasizes dependence on God.

We often think of "disease" as something that strikes us out of the blue, something over which we have no control. This is sometimes true, but more often it isn't. Some of the most common degenerative diseases that plague us—heart disease, strokes, hypertension, most forms of cancer, diabetes—may be at least partly preventable through good nutrition, weight control, regular exercise, and refraining from smoking.

All these conditions are said to involve some genetic predisposition—like alcoholism. And also like alcoholism, they can often be prevented, overcome, or kept under control by self-discipline in changing one's lifestyle.

To put it bluntly, sin is involved in the development of many of our diseases. Gluttony (excessive or unhealthy eating), sloth (lack of exercise due to laziness), and the deliberate pollution of our bodies with poisons such as tobacco are all acts for which we are morally accountable. Yet we don't judge or condemn our loved ones when they bring illness on themselves by such acts. We treat them with compassion, the way Jesus treated the sick.

We also don't deny that a person has a disease on the grounds that his or her behavior was a contributing cause. I've never heard anyone say, for instance, "Lung cancer is not a disease, because Uncle Joe brought it on himself by smoking cigarettes." Yet this sort of reasoning is often applied to alcoholism.

Alcoholism is different only in that it always involves the spirit, mind, and emotions in addition to the body. Treatment in these areas is helpful in any disease or disability, but it is absolutely essential in alcoholism.

So we conclude that alcoholism is a disease, but the alcoholic is still morally accountable for choosing to drink or not or to accept or reject help in overcoming the problem.

Now, it is most important for each of us who is related in any way to a problem drinker to arrive at a good understanding of the "what" and the "why" of what is happening. But the important thing to *you* is that you don't let anything hinder your own recovery from the effects of your loved one's drinking. On the other hand, don't let anyone tell you that your alcoholic husband is not responsible for his behavior because he has a disease. (Would they say that if he were a diabetic who ate pounds of candy every day?) On the other hand, though, don't reject the very real help offered by AA and Al-Anon, among other agencies, just because you think they are "tainted" by viewing alcoholism as a disease, which some of your friends may believe is false.

You and you alone must choose the path to a better life that the Lord shows you, and it will not necessarily be exactly the same as someone else's path. By all means don't let someone else's confusion and misunderstandings hinder your progress.

For Further Reflection

On health, sin, and accountability, read Psalm 38 and 1 Corinthians 3:16–17.

On drunkenness, read Isaiah 5:11–12; Habakkuk 2:15–16; and Romans 13:12–14.

4 *Who Is an Alcoholic?*

It is not good to have zeal without knowledge,
nor to be hasty and miss the way.   PROVERBS 19:2

How can you tell if your loved one has crossed the line between social
drinking and chemical dependency? He may say that he has control
over his drinking, but has he really? I have two short answers for you
and one long one. One short one is, "By the time you have to ask, he
has probably been an alcoholic for some time." The other is, "It
doesn't matter as much as you think. If your life is being ruined by
someone else's drinking, it's more important for you to save
yourself—and improve his chance of sobriety in the process—than to
fool around with definitions."

When I took my friend Julie to an Al-Anon meeting after the
alcohol abuse in her family had brought her to the end of her rope,
she told the members, "I'm really not sure I belong here. I don't know
whether my husband is an alcoholic."

"Yes, you do belong here," several group members told her in
various ways. "If someone else's drinking is messing up your life, it
doesn't matter whether you call him an alcoholic or not. You are not
calling him one just by being here. What you are saying by your
presence is that *you* have a problem with his drinking, and *you* need
some help in handling that problem."

Anyone who looked objectively at Julie's life at that time would
have seen severe alcohol-related problems, not only in her husband
but in their young adult son, too. Yet she was reluctant to call either
of them alcoholics. She loved them! How could she label them with
such a nasty name?

25

Who's an Alcoholic?

To begin the long answer, we need to get back to the problem of defining alcoholism. We have seen the medical definition in the last chapter. One less technical idea on the subject suggests that a person has an alcohol abuse problem when he or she continues to drink even though drinking diminishes the quality of life, whether socially, financially, physically, or mentally. The idea here is that if the drinker were not chemically dependent, he or she would consider the problems alcohol brings to be reason enough to quit.

To put it simply: How important is alcohol to this person? There is a well-known saying that "if you need a drink to be social, you're not a social drinker."

Physical symptoms are usually a reliable sign of growing alcohol dependence, notably buildup of tolerance and the presence of withdrawal symptoms when alcohol is no longer taken.

Tolerance has increased when it takes more alcohol to get an individual drunk than it used to. Some drinkers become proud of their capacity to "hold their liquor," rather than recognizing this as the danger signal it is. A drinker who is criticized for consuming too much, may turn into a secret or private drinker.

Withdrawal symptoms do not have to mean delirium tremens or convulsions. There are milder symptoms like trembling hands, profuse sweating at night, anxiety, and irritability.

In more advanced cases, there are physical signs that do not depend on withdrawal: nausea, vomiting, loss of sexual potence, "beer belly," chronically shaky hands, and a tendency to look older.

Then, too, personality changes are common as the disease progresses. Some of the more common ones are the following:

- A damaged relationship with God and the church, if the person previously was interested in spiritual things.
- Rationalization—always having a good reason to drink.
- Projection—turning self-hatred outward to those closest, with inappropriate anger, bitterness, and far-fetched accusations.
- Mood swings and unpredictable behavior even when not drinking. An alcoholic can go from euphoria to rage without warning

or provocation. Some seem to have a whole different personality when drinking.

- Blackouts—a defect in memory storage in which a person forgets everything that happened during a given period of time.
- Deterioration in job performance—absence, lateness, taking shortcuts, inefficiency, poor judgment. (But the job is sometimes the last thing to go, family life having taken a nosedive long before.)

Twenty Questions

Here is a list of questions widely used by alcoholism counselors. Anyone who answers yes to three or more of these is an alcoholic. Even one or two positive answers spell trouble. Read them, and answer as your loved one might if he or she were being totally honest.

1. Do you lose time from work due to drinking?
2. Is drinking making your home life unhappy?
3. Do you drink because you are shy with other people?
4. Is drinking affecting your reputation?
5. Have you ever felt remorse after drinking?
6. Have you gotten into financial difficulties as a result of drinking?
7. Do you turn to lower companions and an inferior environment when drinking?
8. Does drinking make you careless of your family's welfare?
9. Has you ambition decreased since drinking?
10. Do you crave a drink at a definite time daily?
11. Do you want a drink the next morning?
12. Does drinking cause you to have difficulty in sleeping?
13. Has your efficiency decreased since drinking?
14. Is drinking jeopardizing your job?
15. Do you drink to escape from worries or trouble?
16. Do you drink alone?
17. Have you ever had a complete loss of memory as a result of drinking?

18. Has your physician ever treated you for drinking?
19. Do you drink to build up your self-confidence?
20. Have you ever been to a hospital or institution on account of drinking?

A drinker may try to prove he is not an alcoholic by stopping all drinking for a certain number of days, weeks, or months. Most alcoholics can do this, but it proves nothing. If your spouse wants to test himself this way, give him a real challenge: set a daily limit of not more than two drinks a day for three months. A drinker who can live successfully with that challenge for an extended period of time is probably not an alcoholic. As a rule, an alcoholic loses control after that first drink or two and cannot help drinking more.

Your loved one probably won't agree to try this test just because you ask him to. Or if he does, you may never find out the result.

This Test Is for You

Here is another twenty-question test, but this one is for you rather than the drinker. If you can answer yes to three or more of these questions, your life has been altered enough by someone else's drinking that you should get some counseling for yourself or join Al-Anon or a similar group.

1. Do you spend a significant amount of time worrying about someone else's drinking?
2. Do you lose sleep waiting for the drinker to come home?
3. Do you have health problems related to emotional stress?
4. Is it an unspoken rule in your house that the drinker can do whatever he or she wants, but your needs and desires don't matter?
5. Do you sometimes think you are to blame for the drinking?
6. Do you argue, accuse, or nag about drinking?
7. Is nothing you do ever good enough for the drinker?
8. Has your standard of living been lowered by drinking or related financial problems?

9. Has your social circle narrowed to include only heavy drinkers and their families?
10. Have you missed work or have children missed school because of an alcohol-related crisis?
11. Are you or the children afraid to invite friends home because of possible embarrassment?
12. Has the condition of your home or the level of housekeeping suffered because of drinking?
13. Has the drinker subjected you to verbal abuse, unfair accusations, or irrational anger?
14. Have you been a victim of physical abuse or intimidation by the drinker?
15. Have you taken on responsibilities that properly belong to the drinker?
16. Is your family unable to celebrate a holiday happily or take an enjoyable vacation together?
17. Does the entire mood of the household depend on what is happening with the drinker?
18. Do you think the drinker couldn't get along without you?
19. Do you think your life would be vastly different without him or her?
20. Do you wonder how others manage to live normally?

To Use the Term or Not

Now that you have the two short answers and the long answer, you probably have formed a tentative opinion as to whether anyone close to you is an alcoholic. If not, that's good. But if it seems to be true, it probably is. You are showing courage and honesty in facing this painful fact when it is so much easier to deny it. Please don't feel guilty, as if it were your admission of the fact that made it true. You know that isn't the case.

Next comes the question, should you—now or ever—tell your loved one that you think he or she is an alcoholic? Should you use the word with others outside the family?

Some people feel that the term *alcoholic* is more trouble than it's worth because it is so loaded with negative connotations in our society and arouses so many defensive feelings. They prefer terms that are more emotionally neutral such as "alcohol-troubled person," "problem drinker," or "chemically-dependent person."

I still plan to use the term *alcoholic*, among others, throughout the rest of this book because it has the advantage of being recognized and understood by the majority of readers. I don't believe, as some do, that it is judgmental to label someone else an alcoholic. To me, that is just "calling it as I see it," providing, of course, it's not done in a spirit of anger or blame. Since I believe in the disease concept of alcoholism and genetic predisposition, I don't blame anyone for becoming an alcoholic.

Again, that doesn't mean that any kind of drunken bad behavior is excusable or that you are wrong to get angry over it or that you have to continue living in unacceptable circumstances. Bad behavior can be dealt with separately from alcoholism, and it is not judgmental to recognize it when you see it.

The time may come, however, when you decide to tell your loved one you think he or she is an alcoholic as a means of emphasizing the seriousness of the problem. (Read chapter 7 first.) But make sure you do it gently and in love, not in anger. Know your own motives, for the wisdom writer once said, "All a man's ways seem innocent to him, but motives are weighed by the Lord" (Prov. 16:2).

No matter what words you use to describe the problem in your family, the important thing is to recognize its seriousness and resolve to make some changes in your life that will enable you to be a happier person. It is important that you do this for your own sake, but paradoxically, whatever is good for you is also good for your alcoholic. One expert writes that when the spouse of an alcoholic gets help, the alcoholic has an 80 percent better chance of eventually getting help and becoming sober.

This way, everyone benefits and is happier. The Proverbs writer expressed it well when he said, "A happy heart makes the face cheerful, but heartache crushes the spirit" (15:13).

5 Getting Started in Your New Life

I have set before you life and death, blessings and curses. Now choose life, so that you and your children may live and that you may love the Lord your God.
DEUTERONOMY 30:19–20

Have you become alarmed at the grim future that lies ahead for your problem drinker and your family if things don't change? Did you pick up this book hoping to find the answer to the question, What can I do to make him stop drinking? Please don't give up on me when I answer, "There is nothing you can do to make him stop drinking!"

The chances are that you already know that a frontal assault is futile. Let's face it. How many of the following ways have you already tried?

- Getting rid of all the alcohol in the house
- Begging, nagging, complaining, yelling
- Logical reasoning
- Making "deals" or trade-offs
- Asking friends or relatives not to serve drinks
- Threatening to leave
- Calling or going to bars to coax the drinker home
- Marking bottles, keeping track of consumption
- Searching for hidden bottles
- Taking control of the purse strings
- Getting drunk yourself to "show him how it looks"

Did any of these methods work? For how long? If there were short-term results, were they worth all the trouble?

31

I just have to say at this point that the only "direct" method that has any effect at all is prayer. As you turn the situation over to the Lord, he will give you guidance and good judgment. Remember the old saying, "You can do more than pray, but you cannot do more than pray until you *have* prayed."

The Serenity Prayer used constantly by AA and Al-Anon members, says, "God grant me the serenity to accept the things I cannot change, the courage to change the things I can, and wisdom to know the difference."

There are some things I can change, but there is only one person I can change. That's myself.

"But I'm not the one who needs to change," you may be saying.

With all love and compassion, because I've been there and said that too, I ask you to look again. Haven't some of your own attitudes become bent out of shape through years of living with alcoholism? Weren't there actions you took and decisions you made, at times, that didn't make a whole lot of sense but were reactions to the craziness that was going on around you? Aren't there some positive things you could have done if you weren't feeling too paralyzed and helpless to do them?

Co-alcoholic or *codependent* are terms for someone whose personality has been deeply affected by living with alcoholism or drug abuse. We don't like them, any more than an alcoholic likes to be called an alcoholic. But it isn't a judgment or condemnation, and it doesn't mean we started out different from anyone else. People just change and adjust when living with an alcoholic, because sometimes it seems to be what a person has to do to survive. This is the reason alcoholism is called "the family disease."

It's like a dance. Your partner makes a move, and you move in a way that responds. Then your partner takes another step, and you follow. All of this is beautifully illustrated in the 1954 movie called *The Country Girl*, with Grace Kelly and Bing Crosby. I suggest if at all possible that you obtain a video of this picture, for in it is a classic portrayal of how a "co-alcoholic" acts. In watching it, you may get the feeling they are telling your story.

So, How Do I Change Myself?

In order to change you need to "stop dancing backward!" that is, stop centering your life around your reactions to the actions of the drinker. Since you can't control the drinker, concentrate on regaining control over yourself and taking responsibility for your own actions, decisions, and happiness. To use a different metaphor, you need to drop the reins of your loved one's life and pick up your own.

The important fact is that you can teach yourself to live like a normal person again, whether your loved one stops drinking or not! This may be hard to believe, but it's true. The positive changes you make in your own life may very well be a good influence on your alcohol abuser, but that *must not* be your primary goal. God gave you one life to live on this earth, and your obligation is to live that life before him in a healthy, constructive manner.

In doing this, you will have to make some changes in your underlying attitudes as well as in your actions. It will take time, patience, and self-examination. But the attitudes don't have to come first—your can act your way into better attitudes, and you can start now. These negative forces—denial, obsession, fear, guilt, and so on—are like the "giants in the land" that made the Hebrews afraid to enter Canaan. But of this you can be sure—when you approach them boldly, you'll find the giants aren't as scary as they looked at first, and God will help you conquer them!

Above all, don't waste time blaming yourself for letting your life get sidetracked along with the alcoholic's. If you had known how to prevent it, you would have. Remember, you are smart and you are strong—that's why your alcoholic relies on you so much! So start today to pick up those reins and live your own life. Only you can decide exactly *how.* You and your situation are unique, but in the remaining chapters of this book you will find some specific principles and examples that may be helpful.

Why Should I Be the One to Change?

Maybe you're still asking, "Why me? He's the one with the problem." Here are some of the reasons for you to change.

Change for your own sake. Even if the drinker never changes, there is no sense in two of you going down the drain. If you are a wife, it wouldn't make you a "good wife" to do so. You can become happier, wiser, and more spiritually mature through this experience, but only if you are willing to grow and learn from it. It is true, of course, that there are some people who just wallow in misery and let their problems destroy them—but you don't want to be one of those, do you?

Change to follow the example of Jesus. Jesus was badly mistreated; but instead of showing spite, he set an example of humility and forgiveness that still shines for Christians and non-Christians alike. He didn't just say, "Love your enemies, do good to those who hate you, bless them who curse you, pray for those who mistreat you" (Luke 6:27–28); he *did* it.

Change as an investment in the future of your family. Remember the story Jesus told: you want to build your house upon a rock, not on the sand (see Luke 6:46–49). The emotional interactions learned in an alcoholic family make it more likely that the children will grow up to have troubled families themselves, possibly including marriage to an alcoholic. But when you learn to live in a more stable, positive way, your children will learn too by your example. Even if they are grown, your influence is still stronger than you may think.

Change because you have been given the light. "You are the light of the world. A city on a hill cannot be hidden. Neither do people light a lamp and put it under a bowl. Instead they put it on its stand, and it gives light to everyone in the house. In the same way, let your light shine before men" (Matt. 5:14–16). Right now you may be the only one in your household with enough faith and perspective to be capable of self-improvement. When the others see that you are happier with your new way of thinking and of doing things, they may follow your example.

Elyse's Story

Although Elyse was intelligent and a full-time homemaker, her home was in a constant state of disorganization. Because she had lived with a highly critical and manipulative alcoholic husband for many years, she had almost no self-esteem left. In fact, Max had her halfway convinced that she was "the crazy one." She spent most of her time and energy reacting to him and his demands—dancing backward.

Elyse had come to think she was not, in her words, "a regular person who deserves to live a normal life." She was also ashamed of feeling that way. It was confusing, because she had started out as a very confident and dignified young woman. But when she decided she could no longer continue to live the way she did, Elyse came to realize that you can get to *be* a normal person by *acting* like one, and that you don't have to feel like a normal person to *start* acting like one. You can start with an action and let the feelings follow along later.

Elyse chose the way she was handling the supper hour as her first target for change. It was a time of tension for the whole family, as Max had begun coming home later and later, usually looking for an argument—and he could usually find someone to oblige him. Dreading this time of day, Elyse had taken to starting supper quite late, but this was hard on her hungry teenagers. Then on the occasional day when Max came straight home from work, he was upset because nothing was ready.

One day, she announced to the family that from then on, she would have a well-planned meal ready every evening at 5:30, and she would serve it then regardless of who was at home. After a few weeks, she found that the new system worked very well. It was much easier on her nerves; the children were happier; and most food could easily be kept warm or reheated in the microwave oven for Max or anyone else who was late.

This change worked out so well that a month later she decided to take a further step. When Max came home late, it had been her habit to hover around him, making sure his supper was piping hot and urging him to eat. Somehow she didn't feel her day's work was done until Max ate, even if it was past midnight.

One morning when Max was sober she told him, "I feel too tired at night to stand around, reheat, and serve your supper when you are late. So when the kids and I have finished our dinner, we will leave the food in the kitchen, and you are welcome to help yourself when and if you feel like eating." (Notice that she put this in terms of her own needs. She didn't make a moral issue of it or accuse him of anything. Neither did she ask permission.)

To her surprise Max said, "Fine." Right away she felt happier, more like her old, more confident self. Sometimes she also felt guilty and had to force herself to stay out of the kitchen while he reheated his meal, but she reminded herself that it was alcoholism that made him late, and that she wasn't really doing him a favor by catering to his disease.

One night, though, he tested her and said, "Do you mind getting me something to eat?"

It was very late and she was ready for bed. "Yes, I do mind," she responded. He then went to get a plate, grumbling loudly about "what kind of wife would deny such a simple and basic duty as to feed her man." But the attempted guilt trip didn't work; she felt at peace. She knew that when Max was in a mood to complain, nothing would hinder him from finding something to complain about.

By refusing to make that one small adjustment to her husband's sickness, Elyse had allowed him to behave in a slightly more grown-up and responsible manner. She had given him back a small part of the consequences of his drinking. Ironically, she had done him a favor by doing less for him.

The new system was good for her, too. She had taken up sewing, an old hobby, now that her evenings were more free. Consequently she was happier, and they argued less often. Her new way of life reflected her love for Max—even though she didn't always *feel* loving—better than her insecure hovering had. By helping herself toward happiness, she was hopefully helping him toward recovery.

In thinking about Elyse, ask yourself now what your first change will be. Do something nice for yourself today just because you are important! Stop catering to alcoholism in some small way, and you'll be less angry and self-pitying because you'll have less to be angry about and less to pity yourself for. And in making yourself a little happier, you will be doing something good for that special person you love, too.

Changes That Don't Change Anything

Warning: *superficial changes in your circumstances will have no effect at all on alcoholism!* Regardless of what your alcoholic says, it will not help him quit drinking if you move to the country, if he changes jobs, if you have a child, if you allow your children to live with someone else, if you quit your job (or take one), if you stay away from certain friends or relatives, if you change cities, and so on and on. These kinds of things are called "geographic cures" (humorously) by members of AA and Al-Anon. They know by long experience that they really aren't cures at all.

Though any of these changes might be a good idea for one reason or another, none of them will have any effect on the disease as such. Your drinker doesn't abuse alcohol because of any of the external pressures in his life, no matter what he says. His reasons are deep inside and will remain there irrespective of geographic location.

Wherever you go, there will be liquor. You can't get away from it. Neither can you get away from "those evil companions who are such a bad influence." There are alcoholics everywhere too, and your drinker chooses them as friends because they're his type of people and the kind he wants to be with.

It is also important that you not be isolated from people who are supportive of you, and this could happen if you move away or stop seeing your friends. Far from helping your loved one, isolation helps the disease!

The trouble with so-called geographic cures is that they are an attempt to run away from the problem rather than deal with it. They waste time and their inevitable failure increases your sense of hopelessness. Instead, concentrate on making a change within your own relationship; that's the only kind of change that will lead you to a better way of life.

Expect Resistance

Now, it is important to realize that you are involved in spiritual warfare, and it is serious business. Your enemies are powerful: a disease that has crept into every corner of your family life, and Satan, who wants to keep it that way. But "our side" is even more powerful. First, there is God, and we are assured that "the one who is in you is greater than the one who is in the world" (1 John 4:4).

In addition to God's great power for good, you have more power in this situation than you think! Alcoholic behavior is especially designed to cover up this truth, but it's still true that *your drinker needs you more than you need him!* You not only do a good bit of caretaking, but you may also be your loved one's strongest link with health and sanity. And this is not something taken lightly, because in reality your alcoholic spouse would be thrilled to escape his or her drunken prison. (If there was a decent human being in there before alcoholism, there still is.) So there are three allies: God, you, and the better side of that person you love.

Remember, though, when you start making changes that attack the disease's progress, that part of your alcoholic that is in bondage will panic. He may use a variety of manipulative tricks:

- Respond with great anger to your small changes. (But listen carefully; the anger has a hollow ring.)
- Attack your self-esteem by saying anything he can think of to hurt you. (He knows you so well that he knows just which strings to pull. If you see through this, it will hurt less.)
- Become more arrogant and tell you he doesn't need you, that he could do fine on his own or with someone else.
- "Punish you" by getting drunk more often or at carefully selected times, such as on your Al-Anon night.
- Double up on whatever bugged you most in the past.
- Express a syrupy false sympathy for the "problems" or "illness" troubling you. (The implications are that it's all in *your* head, of course.)
- Stop drinking.

Stop drinking? "Oh, wonderful," you say. "Now I can relax." Not likely; not when it's done without his getting into a recovery program. It will probably be temporary, one more sick game to try to get you to stop whatever you are doing. No matter what—just keep right on with your positive changes. If he really does never drink again, both of you will need some emotional and spiritual recovery just the same. It's okay to be happy that the drinking has stopped; just don't give up your own recovery as part of any related "deal." If your alcoholic is sincere, he'll want you to do what's best for you.

It's important to be patient and move ahead slowly. Your life didn't get off track overnight, and you won't get everything fixed overnight either. Just start with one little step and expect resistance and setbacks, but *don't ever give up!* Each day is a fresh new start, and you can reach your goals because *you are going to regain control over your own life and you are going to become a happier person!* In writing to the Christians in Ephesus, Paul said, "For you were once darkness, but now you are light in the Lord. Live as children of light (for the fruit of the light consists in all goodness, righteousness and truth) and find out what pleases the Lord" (Eph. 5:8–10).

For Further Reflection

On freedom, choice, and responsibility, read Deuteronomy 30:15–20; Psalm 92:12–15; John 8:31–32, 36; 10:10; Ephesians 5:15–17; 1 Peter 4:1–5; and 2 Peter 3:17–18.

On God as your helper, read Exodus 15:13; Psalms 30; 46; 121; Isaiah 41:10–13; and Ephesians 3:12–21.

Part 2 Through Denial to Truth

---

6 Denial: Sweeping It Under the Rug

> Surely you desire truth in the inner parts; you teach me wisdom in the inmost place. PSALM 51:6

Denial is a psychological defense mechanism in which we pretend that an unpleasant truth isn't so. We know, deep down, that it is true, but we are just not ready to face the pain of it. Perhaps you've experienced momentary denial when you were told that someone you cared about had died. "Oh, no!" you said. "It can't be true."

In the case of a death, we soon have to face the truth and get on with our grieving. With alcoholism, it is common to keep on denying for years that the condition exists. Denial is practiced by the problem drinker and by family, friends, even doctors. Alcoholism comes on gradually; its symptoms can be misinterpreted; and heavy drinking is well tolerated in our society. All of these factors make it easier to deny.

Because of denial, alcoholism usually goes unrecognized and untreated until the late stages. The subject is taboo in many homes; many people have grown up with an alcoholic parent and don't realize it until well into adulthood. "I knew my family wasn't normal, but the problem never had a name," they say.

Isn't it odd that families who suffer so deeply from alcoholism are willing to deny the existence of their problem? But it isn't, really. To admit there is a problem is to release all kinds of negative emotions we wish we didn't have. Also, once we "know" such a thing, we are going to feel obligated to do something about it, and we aren't sure what. So for the time being, it's safer "not to know."

How the Alcoholic Denies

Much of the typical alcoholic's denial system is built around exclusionary definitions. In other words, "I can't be an alcoholic because . . .

I don't drink in the morning."
I don't drink every day."
I drink only in bars."
I never drink in bars."
I never drink alone."
I drink only beer [wine, good Scotch, etc.]."
I never drink wine [hard liquor, etc.]."
I drink only with business associates."
I drink only at parties."
I never miss a day of work."
I have friends who drink more than I do."
I've never had a ticket for drunk driving."

All these things are irrelevant. None of them proves that a person is not an alcoholic. Here are some other ways in which alcoholics deny reality:

1. Making excuses for drinking rather than taking responsibility for it. They blame job pressures or a bad marriage or some tragic event in the past. If these reasons were valid, everyone with the same problems would be drinking heavily.
2. Believing they are unloved and unworthy of love, while their thoughts and actions are totally self-centered.
3. Acting in ways that go against their own basic values.
4. Saying they don't need alcohol while centering their entire lives around it.
5. Lying about the amount they consume, sneaking extra drinks when others aren't looking, hiding bottles at home.
6. Failing to recognize that many of their problems at work and at home are caused by heavy drinking, rather than the other way around.
7. Believing a "geographic cure" of one kind or another will help them stop drinking.

8. Believing that "I can stop whenever I want," even after they make sincere efforts to stop and can't.

In the advanced stages, denial may actually take the form of "double-think," or totally irrational and contradictory thoughts. The author Jean Kirkpatrick illustrates this kind of unreal thinking from her own drinking days: "Taking the bottle with me, I went back to the bedroom and drank leisurely, for I had decided that I wouldn't drink that day."

In her book *Turnabout: Help for a New Life*, she also describes deciding never to drink again while taking a few shots as a hangover cure, buying liquor "for guests," and deciding to have "just one" after going cold turkey for days. These are all manifestations of denial.

The alcoholic hangs on tightly to denial because he or she is scared to death of giving up alcohol. It is virtually the sole means of coping with stress and tension.

How You Deny

Congratulations if you have given up denying that you have an alcoholic family member! (I am assuming that everyone reading this book has at least one such person among family or friends. If not, maybe you will be able to help a friend face the disease, and that's good too.) However, don't be hard on yourself for denying in the past; it's normal. We're told that the average family takes seven years to recognize alcoholism after solid evidence exists—and then, usually another two years go by before they seek help.

Here are ways the typical family helps denial along:

1. Believing the alcoholic's denial system. It can be easy to buy your loved one's excuses and rationalizations.
2. Covering up or making excuses to others. "Jim won't be in today. It's a touch of the flu." "Dad is too busy to come to your game tonight, honey. He had to work late." "Don't bother Mom, kids—she's very tired today." "If Lisa acts strange, it's this prescription medicine she's on."
3. Minimizing the problem. "It isn't really so bad. He's such a nice

guy when he isn't drinking. He wasn't always like this. Other people have problems as bad or worse."

As spouses and others who are very close to alcoholism, we have forms of denial that are all our own.

1. We blame the drinker for everything that goes wrong and for his crazy behavior, without taking responsibility for our own sometimes irrational behavior.
2. We think life would be perfect if only he would stop drinking. Look around you carefully—whose life is perfect? Don't wait for sobriety; make improvements now.
3. We think we are controlling the alcoholic.
4. We believe the alcoholic can get better on his own. Almost no one ever does. It takes divine intervention and human help.
5. We think we don't need any help. We think we are superman or superwoman and can handle everything just fine. But there is plenty we can learn from people who have been here before us; besides, it's a blessed relief to find out others understand. Are you reluctant even to bother God with your problems?
6. We think we are already doing as well as we can. Once you take your focus off the drinker and put it back on yourself, you'll be able to recognize your priorities and get back to fulfilling some of your lost dreams.
7. We believe we deserve mistreatment. False, false, false— nobody deserves to be abused in any way. But abuse is so degrading to the spirit that we come to believe it on an unconscious level.

Why You Deny

We have already seen that giving up denial releases negative feelings and forces us to face the question of "what to do about it." But there are other reasons why denial lingers for years beyond its time. One reason has to do with cycles.

Alcoholism tends to get really bad for a while, then better for a time before getting worse again. These cycles are partly a result of the drinker's efforts to clean up his own act. Each new low in behavior shocks and frightens him, so he decides to "get hold of himself," and stop drinking or cut back. And with even limited success comes a feeling of relief that possibly he or she isn't an alcoholic after all. Then after the drinker's guard is let down there comes the danger of lapsing into the old habits.

During the good times, the drinker's false sense of security extends to those close by. Just when you were getting really worried—or angry—the drinker straightens up and looks good for a while. With a sigh of relief you say, "Things will be okay now." But then when the downward spiral begins, you don't want to see it. The disappointment is too bitter.

Rather than send your emotions on a roller coaster ride, try looking at these cycles with a realistic kind of hope. Yes, the good times are a false calm and the bad times get worse. But it's all progress! Your loved one is proving to himself and to you that he can't overcome his condition on his own.

As a spouse, another reason you may not want to face alcoholism in your marriage is the fear that you or the dynamics of your marriage brought on the condition. But alcoholism cannot be caused or prevented by the drinker's relationship with any other person. You never had that kind of power, so let go of that guilt right now.

Another question: Have you denied the disease because you didn't want the humiliation of being pitied? People may offer you pity, but you can refuse to accept it or wallow in it. Walk in dignity, and others will respect you as you respect yourself.

It is important that you let go of others' opinions completely. You may be afraid that people will expect you to do something drastic that you are not prepared to do, like leaving your husband or wife. Or maybe you think people will feel contempt for you if you stay with the alcoholic. Remember, though, that it doesn't matter what they think. It is God you want to please, not people.

At the same time, ignoring a problem doesn't make it go away, even as acknowledging a problem doesn't make it any worse. But giving up the denial tendency can make you *feel* worse temporarily, as you experience the negative feelings you've been sweeping under the rug. The important thing is to get your feelings out in the open. Then they will lose their power over you.

Denial on the Part of Others

After you have coped with your own denial you may still have to face the denial of others among your family and friends. Be patient, however, as you remember that it took time for you to acknowledge the truth.

It's especially difficult when someone else's denial system includes blaming you for the alcoholic's actions. ("Lynn sure makes a mountain out of a molehill." "Dexter must have a lot of trouble at home; otherwise he wouldn't spend so much time in that bar." "My son never drank much before he married that woman." "Mom may drink too much, but she's fun. It's Daddy who acts so weird.") The important thing is not to internalize the feelings and attitudes of others.

Now congratulations on breaking free from denial. In arriving at this place you have taken a huge step in your own recovery. When Jesus said, "The truth will set you free," he was talking about the truth of who he is. But all truth sets us free—free from illusions, from inappropriate guilt, from many kinds of unproductive emotional baggage, free to be whole, healed, and happy. Remember the words of Jesus, "If you hold to my teaching, you are really my disciples. Then you will know the truth, and the truth will set you free" (John 8:31–32).

For Further Reflection

On truth and lies, read Psalm 34:11–14; John 8:44; 14:6; 1 Corinthians 13:6; 2 Corinthians 13:8; and 1 John 1:5–7.

7 Confrontation: Speaking the Truth in Love

Speaking the truth in love, we will in all things grow up into him who is the Head, that is, Christ.   EPHESIANS 4:15

Confrontation is speaking the truth—especially an unpleasant truth—in love. Notice in this verse from the book of Ephesians the two essential ingredients: truth and love. Truth without love is cruel. Love without truth is mindless. Both, of themselves, do more harm than good.

Maybe your mother taught you the same expression mine taught me, "If you can't say something nice, don't say anything at all." Mothers teach this because they don't want to hear their children asking old Mrs. Murphy, "Why does your dog smell so bad?"

But while this principle is all right for casual acquaintances, it's a poor idea to "say nothing at all" when there are problems in our intimate relationships. It is impossible to have closeness without communication, and real communication is not always nicey-nice. To love someone deeply, I have to understand who he is, what he thinks and feels and needs, and how my behavior affects him. In order to love me back, he needs to understand the same things about me.

And to understand, we usually have to be told. Too often, we expect the other person to be a mind reader: "He ought to know how I feel." But how should he know? Not everyone reacts to the same treatment in the same way. We have different temperaments; we come from different backgrounds; and there are basic differences between the sexes. Also, we aren't as sensitive as we could be to body language and other nonverbal signals. We need the words.

Confrontation helps crack through the denial of alcoholism. This may seem hard to believe, but your problem drinker truly doesn't know how his behavior hurts you unless you tell him. Even the average person has to be told, and alcoholics are far more wrapped up in themselves and their own anxieties than the average person. Sometimes they don't even remember what happened after they started drinking on a given day (because of the periods of amnesia called blackouts).

When the drinking problem and all its fallout become unmentionable topics in your home, you are conspiring to protect the disease. Alcoholism thrives in darkness, on all that hush-hush secrecy. Bringing the truth out into the open in a matter-of-fact and loving way can help the alcohol abuser face the fact of the disease and its effect on the family. He or she may eventually become worried enough to want to do something about it. Even without sobriety, you can insist on—and get—better treatment.

Confrontation Isn't Judgment

The Gospel writer gave us these important words, "Do not judge, and you will not be judged. Do not condemn, and you will not be condemned. Forgive, and you will be forgiven" (Luke 6:37). Some people feel that to call anyone else's behavior into question is to "judge" in this negative sense of the word. But I don't think so. I think what the Lord is telling us here is that we are not to condemn anyone as unworthy, inferior, or "no good." When we attack another's basic worth as a person, or declare that we know where he is going when he dies, we are playing God in the most presumptuous and destructive way. Such things are not for us to decide.

It isn't judgment, in that sense, to recognize an obvious sin when you see one. Jesus, Peter, Paul, and all religious leaders down through the ages have done so. In 1 Corinthians 5, Paul advised a congregation to shun a member who was engaged in incest. How could they possibly do that without pinning a label on the sin when it came to their attention? Furthermore, we have already established that drunkenness is a sin, and a grave one at that.

The important thing is to condemn the drunkenness rather than the person who gets drunk. We are to "hate the sin and love the sinner" as the popular expression says. And certainly, a person doesn't have to be blind to sin in order to love.

Judgment interprets the sinner's relationship to God. Confrontation deals with our own relationship to the one who is hurting us.

Judgment blames. Confrontation points out facts.

Judgment assassinates character and denigrates a person's worth. Confrontation deals with behavior, while recognizing the value of the person in God's eyes.

The motive of judgment is to express anger. The motive of confrontation is to express hope for improvement. Judgment throws love away. Confrontation tries to salvage love, heal it, and help it grow.

Forgiveness is a major element of confrontation. After the church member gave up his incest, Paul told the Corinthians to forgive him and reaffirm their love for him (2 Cor. 2:5–11). Jesus gave the woman caught in adultery a second chance, telling her to "go now and leave your life of sin" (John 8:11), while also exposing the hypocrisy of the other, more self-righteous sinners who wanted to put her to death. He did not excuse her wrongdoing in exposing theirs, though.

In Luke 6:42, Jesus says, "First take the plank out of your eye, and then you will see clearly to remove the speck in your brother's eye." Notice the word "first." We are to deal with our own sin first and foremost—and we all have some to deal with. But Jesus never said, "and forget about the speck in your brother's eye." He was warning against self-righteousness, not forbidding his followers ever to deal with someone else's wrongdoing.

How to Confront

Confrontation, when done right, can be a form of peacemaking. It seems ironic, but it's true—when we express our feelings honestly, it becomes possible for us to adapt to one another and live together in greater harmony. We can't change our ways to please our loved ones if we don't know they are being hurt.

When anger and resentment are "swallowed" by one person and allowed to grow and fester in silence and darkness, they can lead to a sudden and total rejection of the other. Many a husband and many a wife have found themselves suddenly alone and said, "I don't understand what happened. Up until the day he [or she] left me, I thought everything was fine between us." How much better to deal with problems as they arise than to have a marriage explode from built-up pressure. Actually, confrontation leads to a real marriage, one with a better chance of survival no matter how severe the problems.

Here's how to go about it:

1. Confront as often as necessary. Deal with important issues as they arise—as soon as you recognize a pattern of behavior that offends you.

2. Pay attention to timing. Morning is usually the best time to confront an alcoholic, as there will be less of the drug in his system. It's useless to talk to a person under the influence of alcohol; he won't really hear you.

3. Stick to the facts. Tell your alcoholic spouse what he did while drunk and how it made you feel. Skip the moralizing, preaching, and predictions of the future. Be specific. Say, for instance, "Last night at Jim and Laura's, you slurred your words, stumbled when you walked, and stepped on their baby's hand. You told Laura her teeth made her look like a rabbit. I felt terribly embarrassed, and also angry with you."

By all means don't say, "Last night at Jim and Laura's you acted like a jerk. I doubt they'll ever invite us there again. Decent people don't want to associate with a drunk." Those aren't facts; those are opinions and conclusions that leave plenty of room for argument. Present the facts, and let the other person form his own conclusions.

4. Make it short and to the point. Say what you have to say in two or three short sentences, at most, and then drop it. Don't repeat yourself or make a long speech. The alcoholic will hear you better

that way, believe it or not. If he acts as if he didn't hear you, he still did.

5. Watch your tone of voice. Keep your voice cheerful and your emotional setting as close to "neutral" as you can. You don't want to sound unduly worried; let the other person decide if there is something to worry about. Don't sound fearful, and by all means, don't vent your anger. You can tell him you're angry, if you are, but an excessive show of emotion might cause your anger to be mistaken for the problem itself: "She's just exaggerating because she's down on me." In fact, any strong emotion from you at this point is likely to harden the position of the other person.

6. Concentrate on "I" messages. Emphasize the effects of his behavior on you by starting your sentences with "I"—for example, "I felt very much alone when you yelled at me and slammed the door."

7. Don't be drawn into an argument. Don't offer a reply if the person disputes your facts or throws counteraccusations at you. It's good to have an "escape route" planned, such as a trip to the supermarket, so you don't have to continue the discussion unduly. Give the other person a chance to think about what you said.

8. Mention any promises he made as if you expect him to remember and keep them: "Oh, don't forget you said you'd take all the kids fishing today" or "How nice of you to offer to install your mother's new roof."

9. You can suggest AA or professional counseling, but don't push for it often. Then, if he agrees, let him make the phone call if possible.

10. Confrontation can be nonverbal. If you find a hidden bottle by accident, put it out in the open. This neutralizes the attraction to "forbidden fruit" and lets the other person know he's not fooling anyone.

11. Praise him, too. Be as free with compliments as you are with confrontation, or more so. Look for something you can truthfully praise, and slip it into casual conversation. If you've gotten out of the habit of doing this, make a point of doing it once a day for the next week. You don't want all your messages to be negative ones.

12. Don't interfere with confrontations by others. Don't be a "big

brother" or "big sister" and jump in to defend your loved one when the drinking behavior causes a conflict with someone else. You may be surprised to catch yourself doing this. Your loyalty is a good trait, but don't misuse it by defending the disease. Such encounters are a natural consequence of the drinking, and it is better to let them take their course. It's healthy for the drinker to face the consequences of his or her own behavior.

How Not to Confront

1. Don't defend or explain any changes you are making. A short, simple statement is enough: "I need all the grocery money for food and cleaning products. From now on, I won't buy beer. If you want it, you'll have to buy it yourself." At the same time, there is no need to analyze your whole decision-making process for him. Let the other person wonder about what is going on in your head. In the same way, don't go into detail about what was said at your Al-Anon meeting or counseling session.

2. Don't try to be the other person's therapist. It's a waste of time to carry on long, late-night, "meaningful" talks about philosophy with a drinker. If you enjoy it, fine. But don't take the "insights" you gain too seriously. And by all means don't try to come up with deep, psychological reasons for the drinking—it only encourages denial.

3. Don't ask why. To ask the alcoholic why he drinks or why he did certain things is to invite excuses and rationalizations. If you are trying to check out facts, ask "what" rather than "why," but even then don't expect the facts to be straight.

4. Don't get involved in disputes about how much he drank or whether he was drunk. You can't win unless you're prepared to do a blood test. Concentrate on the facts you observed for yourself. You can end such a discussion by saying, "Okay, if you had three beers, I guess that's more than you can handle, because you were swerving all over the road."

5. Don't pour out bottles, whether hidden or kept openly. An alcoholic will just find a way to replace them and is sure to rebel

against your attempt to control him or her. And don't play mind games such as searching for hidden bottles or marking bottles.

6. Don't make ultimatums unless you really will follow through. An ultimatum is a strong confrontation that states what the consequences will be if certain conditions are not met. For example, "If I even see you with a drink again, I'm moving out." "If you're not home by seven, I'll go without you." "If you take that child out on the road now, I'll call the police and report you as a drunken driver."

There are times when ultimatums are necessary, but don't overuse or misuse them. First, don't give one unless you are doing it for your own sake (or for a child's sake) and will need to follow through for your own peace of mind. And don't put yourself on the spot by saying you'll do something you aren't prepared to do. But if you do give an ultimatum, don't back down.

Guided Intervention: The Big One

Jesus said, "If your brother sins against you, go and show him his fault, just between the two of you. If he listens to you, you have won your brother over. But if he will not listen, take one or two others along, so that every matter may be established by the testimony of two or three witnesses. If he refuses to listen to them, tell it to the church" (Matt. 18:15–17).

Guided intervention, a technique currently popular among alcoholism counselors, works quite a bit like what Jesus said here. If an alcoholic refuses to listen to the individual confrontations that come his way, he is treated to a carefully planned, "surprise" group confrontation by several of the most important people in his life.

The group can include some combination of the drinker's spouse, children, doctor, minister, relatives, employer, co-workers, and best friend. Participants are chosen for their ability to bring off the confrontation without being judgmental or overly vulnerable; young children should not necessarily be left out, as they can be very effective. The group prepares and rehearses with a professional counselor, who will also be present at the intervention.

When the time comes for the confrontation, each group member in turn speaks to the alcoholic, giving three or four colorful, specific, recent examples of the drinker's behavior that hurt that person. Then following such a confrontation, the alcoholic is asked to enter a treatment program for which arrangements have already been made.

Participants should also tell the alcoholic about any consequences that will occur if he or she refuses treatment. Will she lose her job? Will there be a marital separation, or will a child leave home? Will an old friend decide not to see him anymore? These things should be carefully thought out ahead of time.

Guided intervention is said to have a surprisingly high success rate. Even drinkers who don't immediately accept treatment often change their minds in a day or two. But if that doesn't happen, the intervention shouldn't be considered a failure. It can be a healing and unifying experience for the family because they are freed from the burden of denial—truth has prevailed.

Confrontation is scary. It's frightening to bring hidden feelings out into the open and put them into words. I know. But I believe the benefits outweigh the risks. Speaking the truth in love is tremendously liberating: it will always give you greater inner peace and serenity. Then, too, your loved one's response may be better than you expect. So start in a small way—but do start. The ancient wisdom writer expressed it well: "A truthful witness saves lives" (Prov. 14:25).

For Further Reflection

On confrontation, read Proverbs 12:18; 24:23–26; 27:5–6; Ecclesiastes 3:7; John 8:3–11; Ephesians 4:25; and James 5:19–20.

Part 3 Through Fear to Faith

8 *Be of Good Courage*

Have I not commanded you? Be strong and courageous. Do not be terrified; do not be discouraged, for the Lord your God will be with you wherever you go.
JOSHUA 1:9

The Lord told Joshua not once, but three times, to be strong and courageous as he was preparing for a series of tough battles. Joshua had already shown himself to be exceptionally brave, but the Lord knows that even the most confident of us tend to start trembling when the going gets tough. God's Word is for us, too. The spiritual warfare of living with alcoholism is enough to wear down anyone's fortitude after a while.

How many of the following fears have been yours?

1. That your loved one who drinks might die from it or commit suicide or leave you
2. That you might lose your home or go bankrupt
3. That the alcoholic will embarrass or disgrace you
4. That others will think less of you because you let someone treat you so shabbily
5. That if you try to break free and live a happier life, you will "pay for it"
6. That the alcoholic, in a rage, might hurt you or a child
7. That the general, paralyzing anxiety you feel from time to time means you are going crazy
8. That you will ruin your health through nervousness and worry
9. That something terrible will happen to the alcoholic if you quit rescuing him or her from the consequences of drinking

The first step in getting a handle on your fear is to admit that you have it. If you can identify with one or more of the statements above, welcome to the club—it has a very large membership.

If you do struggle sometimes with fear, anxiety, and worry, be sure to remind yourself—as I do—that courage is not the absence of fear but the wise handling of fear.

Here are some tips for coping that have helped me and others:

1. Take violence seriously. If you or your children are in any real physical danger, remove yourself and them to a safe place as soon as possible. Read the chapters in this book on abuse before going any further. Taking steps to protect yourself doesn't imply personal failure or a lack of trust in God.

2. Turn it over to God. Confess you fear to the Lord as often as you need to, and ask for his help. As you do so, let your feelings of free-floating anxiety come to the surface and wash over you like a crashing wave; don't try to hide from it. Experience the anxiety fully; it may make you shudder, but it won't hurt you. Then say something like this: "Lord, you see what kind of feeling I'm dealing with today. Please remove it from me now and help me to find out where these feelings are coming from and to eliminate the causes."

No, your heavenly Father will not get tired of hearing from you. He wants to help you deal with this and anything else that keeps you from walking fully in his light.

3. Think through your fear. One thing that God will then lead you to do is to cut your fears down to size by examining them completely. Ask yourself, "What is the worst that could happen?"

For example, if you are afraid of going broke and losing your home, you can imagine begging for bread from your former neighbors and sleeping in their toolsheds. Take your scenario to the most ridiculous extreme you can think of. It might make you laugh. Then again, some things will be too grim to laugh at, such as the idea of your loved ones dying. Read the twelfth chapter of Luke, and claim the Lord's promise that he will take care of you no matter what, if you depend on him. In this process you have to give up some of your expectations, but you can trust God to take care of you.

When you have answers for all those pesky "what-ifs," you won't have to dwell on them so much anymore. Your life can only be lived one day at a time, and fears about tomorrow take away from your focus on today. You won't need to picture these "worst-case scenarios" very often, but when you do, remember that that's what they are. They aren't what's going to happen, they're only the worst that could possibly happen.

4. Take action. Sometimes we think we need to have positive feelings first, then do positive things. This is the natural, worldly way to look at it, but God's way is the reverse. We often need to step out in faith—it may feel like "blind" faith, but that's okay—and do some physical thing before God steps in and helps us get the result we want. Good feelings are the eventual result, not the cause or motivation. If Joshua had stayed on the hill overlooking the Promised Land, he could have wallowed there in fear all his life.

Several years ago, an article in a secular magazine for women told of a woman who got through a difficult time in her marriage by "acting as if" she loved her husband. Eventually, not immediately, her love for him returned.

In the same way, you can "act as if" you are not afraid of your alcoholic loved one, of anything he might do, or anything that might happen to him. When you "act as if" you expect that person to take on normal responsibilities, it's more likely—not guaranteed, just more likely—that it will happen.

"Acting as if" can take as many different forms as you have fears. You can "act as if" you hope for your loved one's recovery by praying for her daily, even when she seems to be beyond even the help of God. You can go to bed calmly at your usual time, "acting as if" the missing drinker's whereabouts don't cause you much concern.

5. Don't display fear to the alcoholic. This suggestion is like the last one, because you're going to act as if none of the alcoholic's threats or manipulations affect you in any way. For example, if your alcoholic spouse hints that he'll leave you, don't indicate that you can't get along without him. Or if he says he'll kill himself—wanting you to hover over him—be careful to show no strong reaction. You might say something like, "That would be too bad, but it's your

decision. I can't force you to live. Your life is valuable to me, but it's in your own hands."

Even if the alcoholic threatens your life, it is possible to keep your verbal response calm and neutral. This is not to say that you should take any kind of threat casually. But in any kind of verbal attack, your confident attitude will increase the drinker's respect for you, and threats will grow less frequent. A whipped-dog response on your part just invites more of the same abuse.

"Acting as if" is not being phony or denying reality. You are changing your reality, that's all. Threats are sick, pathetic behavior, and you don't want to motivate the alcoholic to continue to dump verbal garbage on you.

6. Keep busy. Fear is less likely to overtake you when you are engaged in some constructive activity that occupies both your body and your mind. Don't give worry much room in your life. The superwoman described in Proverbs 31:10–31 almost seems too good to be true, but as we read those verses, there's one thing that stands out clearly—she worked too hard to have time to worry.

One evening Brenda decided to clean out, dust, and rearrange her bookcases rather than stew and fret about where her drinking husband was. When Doug came in hours later, she found herself thinking, "Oh, is he home already?"

7. Drain away tension with exercise. Fear, worry, and anxiety build up physical tension in the body. If not released, the tension can make you physically ill. Aerobic exercise is the best kind of tension relief because it accelerates the heartbeat. You can choose any one or more beneficial exercises such as brisk walking, jogging, swimming, cross-country skiing, an exercise or dance class, bicycling, singles tennis, or others. The important thing is to exercise three to five times a week for at least half an hour. But always check with your doctor.

You may also want to drain tension by learning some form of Christian meditation, or conscious relaxation, such as you might learn in a class for prepared childbirth.

8. Watch your diet. Severe panic attacks call for the attention of a doctor. They are sometimes related to the ups and downs of blood sugar—try eliminating sugar and caffeine and eating a nourishing, well-balanced diet.

Dig Out the Roots of Fear

Once you start turning your fears over to God, he may point out errors in your thought life that have caused you to become afraid needlessly. Some of these are listed here.

Thinking It's Up to You to Run the World

Anxiety often comes from taking upon yourself emotional responsibilities that properly belong to God or to others. Remember, you cannot control the actions of others and will never be answerable to God for what anyone else does. It's the same old story—picking up someone else's reins. If you think you *have to do* what you *can't do*, no wonder you feel a little crazy sometimes. Spouses of alcoholics tend to think this way a lot—not only about the alcoholic, but about the world in general. "Let go and let God," as the Al-Anon slogan says.

Overcommitment

Your overdeveloped sense of responsibility may have caused you to take on more jobs than you have the time or resources to do well. Anxiety can come from trying to squeeze twenty-five hours of work into a sixteen-hour waking day. Is this the way you are? How many hats are you wearing: worker, home maintenance, parent, gardener, spouse, volunteer worker, church leader, caretaker of older relatives, foster parent, pet owner, counselor to troubled friends? Stop now and ask God which hats you can hang up for a while. There is just no way you can do it all!

Misdirected Love

The Bible says "perfect love drives out fear" (1 John 4:18). I don't understand exactly how that works, but I think it has to do partly with the fact that perfect love lets go, trusts God, and doesn't try to control anyone else.

Perfect love doesn't demand that my loved one do things *my* way. We can learn this from Jesus. He told—and showed—his listeners how to live abundantly, but he never tried to make them do it right. He wept for them and sacrificed for them (and us) but never did for other people what they were able to do for themselves.

Living More Than One Day at a Time

Regrets about the past and worry about the future cause more unnecessary anguish than almost anything else on earth. "One day at a time" is a slogan central to the philosophy of AA and Al-Anon, but they did not originate the concept. It was Jesus who said, "Therefore do not worry about tomorrow, for tomorrow will worry about itself. Each day has enough trouble of its own" (Matt. 6:34). This does not exclude planning for the future, since the Savior also said to "count the cost" of what we plan to do (Luke 14:28–30). Instead, it is an injunction against stewing about future calamities that may or may not ever happen.

That kind of worrying is called "projecting." I'm sure you've heard about crying over spilt milk; projecting is crying over milk that is still sitting in the pail but might be spilled. A wise person once said, "If you see ten troubles coming down the road, nine of them will hit the ditch before they ever get to you." That is so true. How many things have you worried about that never happened? And, as for those worries that did come true, was your advance worrying of any help?

The only day that truly exists is today. It's up to us to accept this gift with joy and do the best we can with it. And as for the past, it can't be called back or changed. When you have regrets, remind yourself that God's forgiveness is real and permanent. Make amends to anyone you've hurt, if possible, and then put it behind you. Today is the one that counts.

People Pleasing

The fear of "what people will think" is one that often leads to denial of alcoholism. Yet we don't need the approval of people; God is the One who counts. So there's no need to play up to people or put on a show for them.

If you do what is right, your reputation will take care of itself. But if you are sometimes misunderstood, remember God's promise that "an undeserved curse does not come to rest" (Prov. 26:2).

Misunderstanding God

How can God help us conquer fear if we are admonished throughout the Bible to "fear God"? In the first place, it is important we understand that the word *fear* means "to have awe or reverence." In some modern-language versions of the Bible, it is translated "honor" or "respect." This kind of godly fear is not only appropriate, it can even help insulate us against ordinary human fears. If we have the proper awe and reverence for the power of the heavenly Father, and also experience his love, we will have no greater desire than to trust him with full control over our lives. And then, what will be left for us to fear? The psalmist understood this when he said, "When I am afraid, I will trust in you. In God, whose word I praise, in God I trust; I will not be afraid. What can mortal man do to me?" (Ps. 56:3–4).

For Further Reflection

On fear, read Psalms 16; 23; 27; 91; 112; Proverbs 3:5–6; 10:24; 29:25; Isaiah 41:10–13; Luke 12:1–34; Romans 8:15–39; 2 Timothy 1:7; Hebrews 2:14–15; and 1 John 4:16–18.

On living one day at a time, read Exodus 16:1–31; 1 Kings 17:7–16; Psalms 68:19; 90:12; 118:24; Proverbs 27:1; Matthew 6:11, 25–34; 11:28–30; James 4:13–15; and 2 Peter 3:8–13.

9 *Keeping the Faith*

> I have been crucified with Christ and I no longer live, but Christ lives in me.
> The life I live in the body, I live by faith in the Son of God, who loved me and
> gave himself for me.   GALATIANS 2:20

Possibly by now you are saying, "Okay, I won't be guilty of denial,
and I know I've got to make some changes in my life. But it's so hard,
because I'm afraid and confused. I feel alone, and it's easy to slip back
into old ways."

Yes, it is too hard for us alone, but there is help. You cannot
eliminate any negative habit or pattern in your life without substi-
tuting something positive for it. Otherwise, you just leave a large
"hole" in your life and remain vulnerable to the same old problems.
Faith in the living God is what we all need to plug that hole. Faith is
the opposite of fear, and it can occupy the spiritual space that your
fear takes up now.

What is this faith? And how can we get it and keep it while still
living with the chaos and uncertainty that alcoholism brings?

Faith is the belief that God is telling the truth when he says he will
always be with us (Matt. 28:20) and that we don't have to go through
life totally under own own power. Faith is our confidence that God
always keeps his promises. It is trusting the heavenly Father enough
to turn ourselves, our loved ones, and everything we care about over
to him.

The Bible calls faith a gift of the Spirit (1 Cor. 12:9), a shield (Eph.
6:16), and a grafting of our branches into a holy Root (Rom. 11:
17–20).

To have authentic faith, we must take eternal life into account
(Titus 1:2) because God looks at things with a much longer perspec-

tive than we do. We not only live for now but for that future time. In the words of the author of that marvelous "faith chapter" (Hebrews 11), "faith is being sure of what we hope for and certain of what we do not see" (verse 1).

What a relief it is to know that God's faithfulness to us doesn't depend upon our perfection. The life of David as we trace it through his story in 2 Samuel certainly proves that point. In spite of his gross lapses into sin, when he repented, God was faithful in forgiveness. In recording David's dying words, the writer refers to him as "the man exalted by the Most High, the man anointed by the God of Jacob" (2 Sam. 23:1). Yes, our faith is strengthened as we reflect on God's faithfulness.

But faith doesn't just emerge full-blown out of nowhere; it is built up by degrees, step by step. The more knowledge of God's Word we have, the more faith we will have. Then, too, our faith is strengthened as we share what we know with others. You will find it helpful to follow a daily program of Bible reading. And it may help to join a Bible study group and attend an adult Sunday school class. As you become increasingly active in your search for truth, your faith will be strengthened, and you will find it easier to share what you have learned with others.

And, as much as we might hope otherwise, even our problems test and try our faith and make it stronger, if we respond to them correctly (James 1:3–7; 1 Peter 1:6–7). After all, if our faith were never put to the test, it wouldn't mean much. Each problem we face, including those in a difficult marriage or family relationship, should be considered an opportunity for growth and a chance to show the Lord that our love for him is unconditional and cannot be shaken.

How You Can Have It

Wouldn't you like to have the peace and happiness that faith can give you here and now? This is immediately possible, for as we read our Bibles we learn that through Christ's death and resurrection, his salvation is ours as a free gift. All we have to do is accept it. If you have never done so, you can accept Jesus' sacrifice on your behalf right now by saying a simple prayer like this: "Lord Jesus, I know I am a sinner. Thank you for dying on that cross to save me from my sins. I accept your gift of eternal life. Please come into my life, take charge of it, and show me how I can live it for you. Amen."

Possibly, though, you committed your life to Christ long ago but haven't been living like a Christian. If so, now is the best time to rededicate yourself to the Lord. (No matter what you have done, there is no end to his forgiveness.) In taking this step you will find it helpful to read chapters 3 through 8 of the book of Romans.

What Faith Does for You

In addition to overcoming your fears, you will find that your faith in God helps you to live an authentic spiritual life, using your spiritual gifts—special abilities and strengths you didn't have on your own that enable you to help and encourage others.

You will discover that faith is strengthened through use, like a muscle built up by exercise. When your faith is strong and mature, no situation can knock you down for long. You will be always conscious of God's nearness, and his ability to protect you from evil (2 Thess. 3:3). The greatest power in the universe is always with you and in you. The writer of 1 John gave us this promise: "The one who is in you is greater than the one who is in the world" (4:4).

How Faith is Misused

It is important, however, to remember that faith is misdirected whenever it is based on anything other than God. For example, your faith is working against you, not for you, if it depends on any of the following:

- Your own ability to "fix" the alcoholism
- "Wishful thinking" that you can ignore the disease
- The ability of a pastor, therapist, or any human being
- A "geographic cure"
- Your trust that the alcoholic will keep his or her promises

Foolish hopes such as these will set you up for repeated disappointment. And eventually, you will react to the crushing blows by forming a shell—becoming hardened. Perhaps you've already learned, as I did, to protect yourself by deadening your feelings in this way. But how much better it is to trust only God and be open to his miracles.

Yes, God can and does work miracles; he has even sometimes raised the dead. This means there is always hope—hope for a miracle. There are times when the Lord needs our faith to work miracles, although I'm not sure why. We learn in Mark 6:1–6 that Jesus was not able to heal in his own hometown because the people there lacked faith in him. To them he was just "the carpenter."

Sometimes, too, there is some practical thing we need to do before a miracle can take place. When the Hebrews under Joshua were ready to cross the Jordan into their Promised Land, priests had to step into the river before the water would stop flowing and the people could cross safely. And there will be times in your life when it will take a step of "blind" faith to get your miracle.

Faith, Hope, and Love

If faith is our belief in the truth, then hope is the basis on which that belief rests. Nowadays we water down our concept of hope until it means something like "wishful thinking," as in "I hope it won't rain." But the biblical concept of hope is much stronger; it is the confident expectancy, or the active looking forward to *what we firmly believe is going to happen.*

Hope, by definition, is for something we do not yet have (Rom. 8:22–25). Hope is a chance to wait patiently, to prove to the Lord the reality of our faith. Hope is patient but never passive. To hope for your alcoholic loved one's recovery is an act of true love, irrespective of the cost.

Now if faith rests on hope, what does hope rest on? It rests on nothing less than the Lord himself, "Christ Jesus our hope" (1 Tim. 1:1). It rests on his identity and integrity; he always keeps his promises.

Love is said to be greater than either hope or faith (1 Cor. 13:13). But in practice, there is little separation among the three. Faith builds up love, and love helps us to put faith into action. Loving someone who cannot love us back in the way we'd like—someone like an alcohol abuser—helps us understand God better. He loves us unconditionally despite our failures and faults. How can we fail to have faith and hope in the face of such love? In the sixth century before Christ the Old Testament prophet caught the spirit of this when he wrote, " 'The glory of this present house will be greater than the glory of the former house,' says the Lord Almighty. 'And in this place I will grant peace,' declares the Lord Almighty." (Hag. 2:9).

For Further Reflection

On building your faith and hope, read Psalms 31:24; 33:12–22; 119:89–90; Proverbs 3:5–6; Matthew 8; 9; Romans 4:18–22; 5:1–8; Ephesians 2:8–9; Hebrews 6:10–11, 19–20; 11; 1 Peter 1; 3:15; and 2 Peter 1:5–9.

10 *Living the Faith*

Pursue righteousness, godliness, faith, love, endurance and gentleness. Fight the good fight of the faith. Take hold of the eternal life to which you were called.   I TIMOTHY 6:11–12

It seems odd to think of faith as a muscle that has to be exercised regularly, because it is spiritual and not physical. But faith isn't a passive state of being. We don't just sit around and think "faith" to make ourselves feel better. No, when faith is real, it leads to action. Faith becomes faithfulness, or loving action, as naturally as the dawn flows into the day, and we become more like Jesus as we exercise our faith.

Faith starts with the belief that God loves us and is with us always. Jesus would have died for you if you were the only person in the world he could save. We know this because of the story Jesus told of the shepherd and the one lost sheep (Luke 15:3–7). Because this is true, it follows that he wants us to have a decent and productive life filled with dignity, sanity, and healthy, loving relationships. He wants good things for us just as we do for our own children (Matt. 7:7–11).

Faithful people ("full of faith") are godly, loving, humble, open in sharing their beliefs, able to handle responsibility, and willing to serve others. They all serve in different ways because of their unique gifts and abilities. And as you grow spiritually, you will become more faithful and will serve in your own special way.

The book of James, though short, has a great deal to teach us about the way faith expresses itself in action. Above all, it assures us that "faith without deeds is dead" (2:26) and urges us to rejoice in our trials, to love others without prejudice, to tame our tongues, and to do good works. "I will show you my faith by what I do" (2:18).

Good Works

What are good works? They are the things we do that show love to others and meet their needs, whether the needs are physical, spiritual, or emotional. It doesn't necessarily mean giving others everything they want. If your toddler wants to meander into heavy traffic, do you let him do it just because he wants to and is having fun? Of course not! That wouldn't be very loving and it certainly wouldn't be very consistent with the baby's needs.

The love involved in good works sometimes has to be tough love, or love that is motivated by the other person's highest and best good, regardless of what he or she wants at the moment. I firmly believe that tough love, when the motive is right, is a good work. When you enable a person dependent on drugs or alcohol to go right on depending, you are not doing a good work, because you are not considering his or her best interests. (You *enable* when you do anything that makes it easier for the drinker to continue drinking.) It is true, of course, when you refuse to be an enabler, he or she won't be particularly happy about it for a time, but you will be acting out of the very highest form of love.

Suppose that Michelle's husband, who is already quite drunk, asks her to go out and buy him another bottle. On the surface, at first, it might seem like a good work—a good idea—to do what he asks. "After all," she reasons, "that way I can keep an intoxicated driver off the road. And putting myself out to do him a favor shows that I care about him."

But is Michelle really doing her husband a favor? If she consents, here are the results: a few more dollars are spent on liquor; he gets drunker; he is aware that he has asserted an unfair kind of power over Michelle by causing her to go against her own principles; and he loses a little of the respect he has for her.

At such times Michelle needs to examine her motives a little more closely. Is she really making this unscheduled late-night trip out of love, or is it because she wants to avoid the temper tantrum her husband is going to pull if she says no? Could she also be looking for a few extra "moral brownie points" toward her martyr complex?

To use a different sort of example: Ron has decided that a guided intervention is best for his family, and he's in the planning stages. He suffers an agony of guilt because what he is planning doesn't feel very loving at gut level. (Sometimes our gut feelings are wrong.) After all, he is sneaking around behind Tanya's back, planning to say things that will hurt her even though they're the truth, and lining up other friends and relatives to do the same. It doesn't fit with what he's always been taught about a husband's protective role.

Yet look at his motives. He loves Tanya and wants her to recover from the fatal disease of alcoholism. Ron wants to save their marriage and to build a strong family. And although he can't quite *feel* it yet, he knows he is displaying a high form of love, as well as commitment to his wife's best interests.

It may seem paradoxical, also, that our faith requires that we be willing to surrender our loved ones completely if necessary, as Abraham was willing to sacrifice Isaac in obedience to God's instructions (Gen. 22:1–18). For example, Michelle has to "let go" enough to risk her husband's displeasure by not going as he asks. And Ron has to cope with his fear that the intervention will make Tanya so furious that she'll leave him. Love has its risks. We have to be able to pray, "Father, I want that special person healed, and I want us to be happy together. But whatever you decide, no matter what, it's okay with me."

This kind of faith is what it takes for a miracle to happen. There are many people alive today who have seen their loved ones healed and delivered from all sorts of "hopeless" conditions after praying that way. Even if there is some reason why our desire can't be granted, our prayer strengthens our relationship with our Father.

Two Warnings

Two warnings come to mind at this point. One has to do with the currently popular teaching called the "prosperity doctrine." According to advocates of this idea, if your faith is strong enough, you should be able to get anything you want automatically—healing, miracles, wealth, or whatever. According to this theory, only a lack of faith can keep your prayers from producing spectacular results. But to accept this false idea is to treat God like some kind of giant vending machine in the sky! We are to conform to *his* will, not the other way around.

Sometimes God wants us to wait and lean on him more. There are times when he may say no, although our pain hurts him, because of some larger plan he has for us. God sees beyond the immediate moment.

The other possible danger lies in letting our "head knowledge" get too far ahead of our ability to put what we believe into action. There are times when we want to soak up all the knowledge we can from Scripture, sermons, books, tapes, seminars, and other sources. But doing it without putting into practice what we already know can lead to discouragement. It's like trying to lose weight by reading lots of diet books (my former practice).

It is important that we balance our learning with *doing*. This means that when you come across a biblical teaching that looks as if it may be helpful, make plans right away to apply that idea to your own real life situations. Our best help for daily guidance comes through reading God's Word—the Bible—and praying. The Holy Spirit will guide us into the truth.

How Should We Pray

The importance of prayer as an exercise of faith cannot be overestimated. Along with your other prayers, you should pray especially for your alcoholic loved one every day. Sometimes it will be the only constructive thing you can do.

Choose a daily quiet time when you can be alone and undistracted. Early morning is often good, or naptime if you have small children. In my experience, bedtime is not good because sleep comes too easily. But it can be a good time to touch your sleeping spouse and pray for him or her. In addition, use odd moments for prayer during the day—while driving, doing physical work or exercise, in line at the supermarket, or when waiting for someone. And at times you may find it helpful to pray with a partner, especially someone more mature in the faith.

Here are suggestions on what to pray for and how to do it:

1. Start with praise and thanksgiving. Praise God for who he is and for all he has done for you. Praise him for protection, personal growth, material things, health, family, friends, and small everyday pleasures.

2. Confess your sins and ask forgiveness. Accept God's ready forgiveness. Ask him to bring to mind any wrongdoing you may not be aware of, as well as any amends you need to make to anyone. (Amends are anything you can do to help make up for the hurt you have caused another; see Matt. 5:23–24). Unconfessed sin is a barrier between you and God.

3. If you want to be forgiven, you in turn have to forgive anyone who has hurt you, including your alcoholic loved one. Ask for enough faith to be able to forgive (see Matt. 6:12 and Luke 17:3–5).

4. Now, and only now, are you ready to start asking favors. It's appropriate to ask for healing for a loved one on the basis of your own faith, not necessarily his. (See Matt. 8:5–13 for an example.) Rely on the Holy Spirit to guide you in what you ask for. You don't always have to be saying words when you pray (Rom. 8:26–27); sometimes you'll be listening. Answers will come through the Spirit, usually as distinct impressions on your mind rather than as an audible voice.

5. Whatever you ask for, ask "in the name of Jesus Christ the Lord" (see John 16:22–27). Jesus intercedes with God the Father on our behalf and wants us to ask for good things in his name.

6. It is essential to ask with the right motives—for the glory of God and the enhancement of his reputation on earth. The writer of the book of James tells us that we won't get an answer if our purpose in asking is for our own selfish pleasure (4:3).

Of course, there is nothing wrong with asking for a person or a marriage to be healed. Spiritual growth in a person is always gratifying to God. Your motives make a real but subtle difference.

7. Pray that the strongholds of Satan will be torn down in your alcoholic's life, even in his thought life (2 Cor. 10:3–5).

8. If your alcoholic has never accepted Jesus as Lord and Savior, make that a primary focus of your prayer. Other good things will follow from that. Pray that all the little spiritual "seeds" that you and others have planted will sprout and grow.

9. Pray for more love for your alcoholic loved one and for appreciation of his or her better qualities. If your love is not strong, read John 15:9–17, and ask for God's love to abide in you.

10. Pray with faith, knowing that "all things are possible with God" (Mark 10:27). And pray that your faith will be increased day by day.

11. Pray boldly and don't be afraid to claim the promises of God for your situation. Claim the promises in God's Word. There are hundreds of such promises; a good one to start with is found in Luke 11:9.

12. Pray persistently. Sometimes we may feel we are "nagging God" when we keep asking for certain things over and over again. But we read in Luke 18:1–8 that God wants us to keep asking. It's not that he needs to be convinced of what's right; he just wants to know how serious we are.

In God's wisdom, the Almighty wants us to help accomplish his plan here on earth through prayer and good works. And in fulfilling his purposes for us we will grow spiritually as we strive with his help to defeat the Enemy. Jesus asks in Luke 18:8, "when the Son of Man comes, will he find faith on the earth?" It is important that we do our part to make sure he does!

For Further Reflection

On faith and faithfulness, read Proverbs 3:3–8; Matthew 8:5–13; 25:14–30; Luke 8:40–56; 1 Thessalonians 5:23–24; and James 1:2–8, 22–27; 2:14–26.

On God's promises, read Psalm 37 and Matthew 5:3–12; 7:7–12; 11:28–30.

On prayer, read Matthew 6:5–15; Mark 11:22–25; Luke 6:27–28; 1 Thessalonians 5:16–18; James 5:13–18; and Revelation 5:8.

Part 4 Through Obsession
to Detachment

11 *Let Go and Find Peace*

Great peace have they who love your law, and nothing can make them stumble.

PSALM 119:165

Do you "stumble" over references like the one above in Psalm 119 that speak of the peace of God? "How can I have peace," you wonder, "when my life is inextricably bound up with that of someone who wants nothing to do with peace? I'm always picking up the pieces after some crisis."

Yes, the daily, petty irritations of living with an alcoholic can seem like the slow drip, drip, drip of some kind of torture. Then when the big blowouts come, you have no reserves of emotional strength and so are completely drained. And possibly you feel unhappy and trapped even though you can still find things to love about your drinking loved one. Could it be that your preoccupation with him or her borders on obsession?

Consider the lyrics of the popular love songs we have heard all of our lives. They say things like, "Oh baby, I can't live without you. I think of you all day long. I'm nothing without you, and if you were to leave me, I'd just curl up and die." This attitude elevates romantic love to a form of idolatry, and seems actually to invite cruel treatment. Yet, this is the way our culture teaches us to think.

Well, here's the good news: the hold your alcoholic loved one has over your mind and emotions is potentially under your control. You can, and must, cut it down to a more manageable size, and the process of doing this is called detachment.

Now, detachment doesn't mean that you stop caring about your loved one. Instead, it means that you hold your emotions back from

79

overinvolvement. You give him or her the proper amount of time and attention, but not a lot more.

If you are the wife of an alcoholic, call to mind some woman you know in a good, "normal" marriage. (If your alcoholic is your grown child, think of some parents of "normal" kids, and so on.) Then ask yourself if these "normal" people appear to spend all their time worrying about their loved ones and what they're going to do. Do they appear to be obsessed about the meaning of every little action and comment? No, of course not! They live their own lives, and you can too!

"That's easy to say," you may be thinking, "because these normal people are more secure in their relationships. They haven't been put through the wringer the way I have." True; but you too can live more normally. Affirm this truth every day.

How Obsession Develops

The manipulations and power games that are part of alcoholism are designed to keep the thoughts and energies of loved ones confused, focused exclusively on the drinker, and dedicated to enabling the drinking.

The abuser of alcohol typically uses anger and intimidation to keep the spouse and other family members in line. These ploys are especially effective with wives—although they are successfully used on husbands, parents, and children of drinkers as well—because the wife is culturally conditioned to want to please her husband. She tries to do whatever her husband wants and to avoid the angry outbursts of verbal (even physical) abuse that come when he is displeased. But because his desires are unpredictable, it becomes more and more difficult to please him. Family members keep trying, though, believing, hoping that "If only I could meet his needs perfectly, maybe he wouldn't drink."

Then, too, the alcoholic plays on the family's guilt and fear. Eventually the unwritten rule of the family becomes "Daddy's every whim is our law." Everything revolves around the moods of the drinker; no one can make plans, because they may have to be changed at the last minute. At the same time the alcoholic's attitude becomes "I'll do whatever I want, and you'll do whatever I want, too."

When the husband and father is the alcoholic, this domination goes far beyond what God intended for him as the spiritual head of the home. Loving, sacrificial, Christ-like leadership is God's standard for a husband—not a petty tyranny that confuses the husband with God himself.

Children with an alcoholic parent either keep trying to be perfect or they give up and withdraw from family relationships, becoming "invisible." Another response of children is to rebel, perhaps taking on drinking, drugs, and delinquent behavior themselves.

Guilt and fear can lead one to ridiculous extremes in trying to please a drinker. Connie's husband told her he drank because there was never good food on the table. In response to that accusation Connie resolved to always have a good meal ready whenever Dave was hungry.

Like a petty tyrant Dave set the time when he wanted his dinner. And the menu had to be adjusted to fit his moods. If a roast was half cooked and Dave wanted pork chops—goodbye roast. Or if he decided he'd rather eat out at a restaurant, they'd leave dinner in the oven.

Do you think this "demand feeding system" helped Dave to drink any less than before? Hardly. There was never any shortage of reasons why he needed a drink.

This type of husband does whatever he can to make his wife feel insecure. He often flirts openly with other women and threatens during an argument to walk out and not come back. Then, too, this kind of husband plays up his wife's faults in an effort to make her feel small and inadequate. By contrast, a "normal" husband wants his wife to feel beautiful, secure, and loved.

Sometimes, though, the domineering alcoholic husband will unpredictably treat his wife like a queen for no apparent reason. He buys her an expensive gift and praises her, saying, "You're wonderful to put up with me the way you do." This is even more addicting to her, of course. "He really does love and appreciate me," she thinks. But deep down, it doesn't satisfy. She wants to be treated decently on a regular basis and loved for who she is, not for what she "puts up with."

This sort of thing happens when the drinker is the dominant personality in the family. On the other hand, sometimes the alcoholic is the marital partner with the more gentle temperament; in that case the dynamics are different, although not any healthier. The alcoholic just becomes sneakier about the drinking. Many a quiet alcoholic housewife keeps liquor in bottles that look like a household cleaner or medicine. And she cuts down on other expenses to disguise the amount spent on alcohol.

When the drinker is a mild-mannered man, the wife may similarly feel that she is in sole charge of the family, although she is just as obsessed with her husband's comings and goings as her meeker counterpart. She is also just as likely to take over his responsibilities. Consequently, when he gets drunk or she discovers his hidden bottles, he takes on the air of a "bad boy" rebelling against a strict mother. And her anger and scolding absolve him of his guilt feelings.

In almost all alcoholic families, there is a warped sense of who is responsible for what. Danny gives Margaret his entire paycheck every week. She, the sober one, is supposed to pay the bills and hide the rest of the money so that he can't go out drinking. If he finds the cash and blows it, that is her fault, they both think, for not hiding it well enough.

Serenity Through Letting Go

Even as faith and hope are antidotes to fear, they should also dispell any ideas we might have that we can control another person's destiny.

There is powerful truth in the prayer-petition "God grant me the serenity to accept the things I cannot change." One of the primary things you can't change is your alcoholic's freedom of choice. You cannot have a healthy relationship without accepting the fact of the other person's free will. Even child rearing is a process of gradually releasing control over the child's life and decisions. If we cannot— and should not—dominate the lives of even our older teenagers, how much less can we expect to make choices for another adult?

The other side of the coin is that if we can't make decisions for another person, neither can we be held accountable for his or her actions. It is obvious this truth isn't understood when we hear a person say, "Don is in rough shape. You just must do something about him!" But true acceptance means knowing in your heart where your responsibility begins and ends—what you can and can't do. When you accept, you can see things as they are.

Not only are we to accept the things that cannot be changed, but as the prayer urges, we are to have the "courage to change the things we can." What you can change is your own reaction to your circumstances. You are responsible for your own life, including your thought life. Your happiness doesn't depend on your spouse or any other person; you aren't being disloyal if you reach out for a little happiness of your own. You don't have to wallow in your alcoholic's misery.

The prayer concludes with this significant petition for "wisdom to know the difference." If letting go boils down to "minding your own business," it takes special insight to determine what is your business. Letting go doesn't mean just giving up in apathy and defeat. Rather, it means taking action only after we have thought through a problem, asked God for guidance, and determined what is the best and most loving thing to do. God wants us to use the brains, free will, and wisdom he give us.

How to Detach

"Detachment" means disengaging your emotional overinvolvement with your alcoholic and the situations he or she gets you into. It means not becoming obsessed, and it means making your own decisions calmly. Of course, it's one thing to talk about detachment and quite another to practice it in the heat of a crisis—when the drinker has wrecked the car, failed to show up for an important event, or spent two straight hours telling you how worthless you are.

At such times it will help to get alone even for a minute or two and repeat to yourself the Serenity Prayer, a favorite hymn or Bible verse, or an Al-Anon slogan such as "Let go and let God," "Easy does it," "First things first," or "One day (hour, minute) at a time."

Try to respond calmly even when the alcoholic and others are angry or upset. Don't let anyone coerce you into making a decision you're not ready to make. If someone is trying to manipulate or bully you into something, say, "I'm not ready to talk about that right now. I'll get back to you when I've had a little more time to think."

If verbal abuse is getting you upset, remember to mentally label it for what it is: "This is the alcohol talking. I won't take it personally."

Or, take some mental "time out" to admire something in your immediate surroundings that is beautiful: the shape of a baby's head, a single flower, the pattern of clouds in the sky. No matter where you are, there is beauty.

Above all stop keeping track of your drinker's consumption of alcohol. Counting his drinks and looking for hidden bottles are acts that help keep you obsessed. Remember, he isn't "getting away with it" if there are drinks you don't know about. Consequences have a way of showing up on their own.

However, detachment doesn't mean maintaining a grim silence. There are times to be quiet and times to confront. Detachment is just a calm state of mind that helps you decide wisely which is which.

Once when I was waiting outside a tavern for my husband—a situation that would sometimes make me angry and resentful—I just put my head back, looked up through the windshield, and watched the sunlight filtering through a thick screen of maple leaves. The play of light and the various shades of green were so beautiful, they truly made me forget to feel bad. When someone came out to ask me to "join the fun," I replied that I was happy where I was. And it was true.

Remember, though, that you have to give freedom in order to get it. Part of my serenity at that moment came from the knowledge that I could leave anytime I got tired of waiting. My husband could have found another way home. This thought relieved me of any pressure I might have felt to make him come home with me.

Your mind is the key to abundant life. As we read in Philippians 4:8, "Whatever is true, whatever is noble, whatever is right, whatever is pure, whatever is lovely, whatever is admirable—if anything is excellent or praiseworthy—think about such things." Your mind is under your control, and if you choose to think about positive things *most of the time*, you will have happiness and peace. You won't be obsessed with a problem over which you have no direct control.

But God cannot take control of your problems while you are still tightly grasping them. Turn them over to him, and he may come up with solutions you could never have thought of on your own. One thing's for sure—the Lord wants you to have the serenity that comes from letting go of what is not yours. Only then can you think clearly about what, if anything, you need to do. Let go, and accept your serenity as a precious gift from him. Fix your thoughts on these words of Jesus, "Peace I leave with you; my peace I give you. I do not give to you as the world gives. Do not let your hearts be troubled and do not be afraid" (John 14:27).

For Further Reflection

On peace and freedom, read Psalms 85:7–13; 146:7; Proverbs 14:30; Isaiah 26:3; Romans 12:18; 2 Corinthians 3:17; and Galatians 5: 22–23.

12 *Let Go of the Consequences*

The soul who sins is the one who will die. The son will not share the guilt of the father, nor will the father share the guilt of the son. The righteousness of the righteous man will be credited to him, and the wickedness of the wicked will be charged against him.   EZEKIEL 18:20

Just as each of us makes decisions, we must also take responsibility for what we do and live with the consequences of our actions. If the results are good, we're more likely to make similar decisions in the future. If the consequences are not good—if we are "punished" in some way for what we do—we learn to avoid that kind of behavior in the future. Either way, we learn from our own past conduct. The wisdom writer said it well: "If a man digs a pit, he will fall into it; if a man rolls a stone, it will roll back on him" (Prov. 26:27).

Yes, other Bible verses say that the consequences of sin can remain with a family for three or four generations. This is just something that happens naturally and is not a deliberate punishment inflicted by God. The person committing a wrong act is the only one to be held morally accountable for it, although innocent parties sometimes suffer along with him or her.

This natural order of things becomes distorted in the alcoholic family, as other family members begin to try to assume the drinker's negative consequences and shield the drinker from the pain caused by his or her behavior. But when this happens the drinker doesn't learn anything from the mistakes, doesn't come to realize how harmful his or her actions have been.

By "rescuing" the alcoholic from the consequences of drinking and poor behavior, we actually get in God's way; we interfere with the drinker's relationship with God and help keep his conscience from functioning properly. When others suffer all his pain for him, he has no motivation to change.

So, do we need to "punish" the alcoholic to get him to learn what he is doing wrong? No. All we need to do is step out of the way and let things take their natural course. The important thing is to avoid jumping in and rescuing the alcoholic.

For example suppose that Fred has been out drinking one summer night and he doesn't quite make it into the house but passes out on the front porch. His wife, Janet, could haul him bodily inside, clean him up, and put him to bed. But that isn't something a wife should have to do. If Janet does look after him that way, she is suffering for his decision to get drunk. How about Fred, though? Is *he* inconvenienced or suffering? No—he wakes up warm and dry in his own bed, just as if he'd behaved responsibly. He hasn't learned a thing from his previous night's episode that would keep him from getting drunk again.

On the other hand, suppose Janet lets him spend the night out on the porch sleeping it off. In the morning when Fred comes to, he hurts all over, smells bad, and is self-conscious knowing that his early-rising neighbors have seen him stretched out grotesquely on the porch. Now he has learned what can happen as a result of his picking up that first drink. It is true he may be angry at Janet for not rescuing him, but he has no legitimate gripe with her. It was his actions, not hers, that caused him to sleep on the porch. Although he may accuse her of being cold and heartless, she has actually acted lovingly. She loves him enough to want to help him get well.

What Kind of Love Is Tough Love?

We defined tough love in chapter 10 as love that is motivated by the other person's highest or best good. In practice, tough love often means allowing the loved one to suffer the consequences of wrong actions. You don't take on the other person's punishments. You don't accept unacceptable behavior, but instead you hold him accountable.

Does that sound mean and cold? It isn't. It doesn't involve "giving up" or washing our hands of our alcoholic loved one, and it certainly doesn't mean we no longer care what happens to him or her. Rather, it means we care enough to let go and respect that person's individuality and freedom of choice. Tough love isn't easy; we suffer quite a bit of emotional discomfort in learning to practice it, as we work through the crippling guilt and fear that have kept us in the role of rescuer.

Ironically, the practice of tough love can make the alcoholic begin to want to get well. When the family stops centering around the drinker and constantly taking his pain for him, a kind of pressure builds up in him that may evoke a desire for sobriety. Tough love raises the drinker's self-esteem to a healthier level as he takes on more personal responsibility. Also, when you appear to quit worrying about his health and welfare, he may develop more concern for it himself. At the same time, he will respect you more as you show more self-confidence and stop hovering over him.

In addition, your good feelings about the alcoholic will increase when you develop a healthy amount of detachment. You'll have less reason to resent him or her when you are taking better care of yourself, and you'll be able to better appreciate your loved one's good qualities. Sometimes we hover and rescue because we feel guilty about our resentment of the drinker and are afraid we don't love him or her anymore. But as a more normal balance is restored to your relationship, you'll find the alcoholic actually doing things to try to please you.

Tough love is biblical, godly love. God gave us free will—he takes the risk that we will make bad decisions. He could have made us totally controllable, like robots, but then our love wouldn't mean much to him, would it? In the same way, we must give those we love their freedom even though we risk losing them.

Jesus also "let go" lovingly. Did he prevent the rich young man from walking away? (see Mark 10:17–23). No, the man was allowed to decide for himself and to live with the consequences of his choice. Jesus didn't do for others what they could and should do for themselves. The only reason he died on the cross for us was that we were totally incapable of atoning for our own sins. Even now we read that he "stands at the door and knocks" (Rev. 3:20). He doesn't barge into our lives and take over, although it's a fact that he could manage things better than we do.

Watch your motivation as you practice tough love. You should want the best long-term benefit for your alcoholic loved one—if you just want revenge or to "demand your rights," that isn't love. The difference is subtle but very real. Think about what you would want your loved ones to do if you were the one engaging in self-destructive behavior. Even as you take tough actions, or refuse to engage in rescuing, you can maintain an attitude of forgiveness.

How Does Tough Love Work?

It isn't the purpose of this book to tell you exactly what to do. You are capable of making your own decisions, and you know your situation better than anyone else. Also, you may not be emotionally ready to take a certain action that you believe is right. That's all right; give yourself time. However, here are some things "tough love" has meant to others:

- Let the drinker find his or her own way home at night.
- Refuse to call in sick for a worker who is hung over.
- Stop paying bills that are the alcoholic's responsibility.
- Stop interfering in the drinker's arguments or misunderstandings with other people. Stop apologizing for him, since an apology implies that you are partly responsible.
- Let a drunk driver spend a night in jail rather than putting up bail immediately.
- Tell the truth about the source of an injury rather than protecting a physically abusive alcoholic.
- Confront the drinker about the drunkenness, using a guided intervention if necessary.

Yes, it's true that an alcoholic may make mistakes—even very serious and costly ones—when you reduce your caretaking activity and start letting him make more of his own decisions. But don't let guilt get to you. Any bad decisions are his, not yours. After all, your hovering hasn't prevented mistakes in the past. His mistakes may cause him to "hit bottom" and want to get sober. Remember, caretaking and rescuing will prolong the disease.

Don't be threatened by feelings of fear either. Are you afraid your alcoholic spouse will leave you or cut off his or her ties to you if you stop rescuing? If that were the case, you might well be better off without him. But generally it doesn't work that way. He will respect you more as you respect yourself more.

Question: If alcoholism is a disease, doesn't that mean that the person who has it needs extra loving care and protection? No. More personal responsibility is a better prescription for an alcoholic who is not doing anything to try and recover. Tough love does protect; it protects against the harm that can come to a whole family when alcoholism is allowed to flourish unchecked.

For a sense of balance, frequently read the Bible's great "love chapter" (1 Cor. 13). There you will be reminded that love is patient, kind, and humble. It is not envious, boastful, rude, self-seeking, easily angered, or unforgiving. You can cling to these positive attitudes even as your love takes on the "toughness" it didn't have before.

As your alcoholic loved one sees you becoming less and less involved in your rescuing behavior, it is possible he or she might conclude that you simply don't care anymore. If this happens, I urge you to continue to find ways to express your love without violating your tough love principles. You can do it by learning to hear and speak your dear one's own "love language."

Actions that say "I love you" vary from person to person. One man "hears" his wife say "I love you" when she irons his shirts to perfection, while another man doesn't care so much about shirts but hears "I love you" when his wife wears her hair the way he likes it. One woman hears "I love you" when her husband uses his vacation time to paint the house. Another woman feels love when her husband makes her a special cup of hot tea when she is suffering from a cold. Whatever seems to make your loved one especially happy and grateful—flowers on the table, a home-cooked meal—that's what you can do to make him or her feel loved, even as you take a tough stand on drinking.

Tough love is a lot of work, spiritually, but you can do it—you can keep the toughness without losing the love. Remember the Apostle Paul's words to his Christian friends in Rome. "Love must be sincere. Hate what is evil; cling to what is good" (Rom. 12:9).

For Further Reflection

On love, read Matthew 5:43–48; 22:37–40; John 15:9–17; Romans 12:9–21; 13:8–10; 1 Corinthians 13; and 1 John 4:7–21.

On responsibility, read Ezekiel 18.

13 *Anger: Detoxify the Poison in Your System*

> In your anger do not sin. Do not let the sun go down while you are still angry, and do not give the devil a foothold.   EPHESIANS 4:26

If you had asked me two years ago, I would not have admitted that I was angry with my husband. I was putting up with some treatment I didn't like, but I seldom told him how I felt about it. After all, he should know, shouldn't he? I sometimes confided my troubles to close friends, and I attended meetings of Al-Anon and a Christian self-help group. In all these discussions, I tried to remain upbeat and positive in all I said. I had to show everyone what a "good Christian" I was and how self-controlled. I was so busy being "spiritual" that I couldn't allow myself to be real.

Then one day while out walking with a friend, I surprised and upset myself by "blowing my cover." I complained long, hard, and bitterly to this dear woman. Why her? Why then? I knew her own background, and I suppose I sensed, correctly, that she would understand and not judge me.

After that I had to admit to myself that I was sitting on a lot of bottled-up anger. I knew that wasn't good; a spirit that holds in a negative emotion for a long time is like a body that is constipated. The waste products are a burden on the system and need to be eliminated. But I didn't know what to do about it.

This is what I wrote at that time on an index card that I put in my Bible, "What is the correct thing to do with anger so I am not 'stuffing it' inside? Does turning it over to God mean expressing it only to him, or does it mean he will show me what to do with it? Is it a sin to get angry because my own high hopes and expectations are violated?"

After some thought and prayer I decided to confront my husband with my anger. He was so hard to pin down, I had to make an appointment with him at his place of business. I told him how some of his recent actions had hurt and angered me, and I suggested that we both get some counseling. After doing this I felt better immediately, even though his first reaction was anger.

In the following weeks, he referred to that conversation several times and made some positive changes. I thought it was wonderful just knowing he had heard me.

Deal with Anger Constructively

My prayer and reading—in the Bible and other sources—has convinced me that anger is not wrong in itself, and it certainly is not wrong to express it in a good confrontation. When anger becomes long-term, inward rage, it poisons both body and soul. It blunts our capacity for more desirable feelings, like love, joy, and peace, and it causes us to be alienated from the very ones with whom we want to be close. It is important that we learn how to neutralize this poison.

As Christians, we often ask ourselves whether we have "the right" to feel certain negative emotions, and we tend to go off on guilt trips over feelings we see as "wrong." But I now believe that our feelings at any given moment are not moral issues in themselves. They are not right or wrong, they just are, and God accepts us as we are. But because anger and other negative feelings are harmful to us, we have to learn how to deal with them constructively.

However, anger is not all bad. It can be useful when it helps us face a bad situation and make necessary changes based on scriptural standards. Constructive anger can help us take a stand against a wrong, defend an innocent victim, protect a child from danger, or begin to reject the consequences of someone else's bad behavior. (Anger *could* be a sin if it served only our own convenience or selfish desires.)

We read in the Gospels that Jesus was angry at times. In the Old Testament, we see God the Father getting especially angry at the sins of the people he loved best. He describes himself as "slow to anger" (Exod. 34:6), and the condition is temporary, "For his anger lasts only a moment, but his favor lasts a lifetime" (Ps. 30:5).

We need to accept our anger (not deny it, as I did) and learn how to express it appropriately. Before confronting the alcoholic loved one or anyone else, consider carefully your true feelings. Sometimes we are angry at someone and take it out on "innocent bystanders," especially children. It is sometimes true that we give others angry messages "in code" because we haven't accepted our real motivation. For example, Gail kept telling her husband, "You don't spend enough time with the children," when she really meant, "I need to know whether you still care about me."

As you already know, I'm sure, confrontation is not the same as "ventilating" your anger. Shouting, arguing, name-calling, and stony silences do more harm than good. They make the recipient angry at *you* and invite retaliation. Then instead of the two of you being reconciled, your position as "enemies" becomes more fixed. Also be careful how you involve a third party. You may have a legitimate need for some counseling in dealing with your anger, but indiscriminate complaining and sarcastic "joking" to others are absolutely out, of course.

Acceptance Reduces Anger

It's good to acknowledge and deal with anger, but it's even better not to let it get a hold on you in the first place. Acceptance is the key to prevent this from happening.

Acceptance is the recognition that "what is, is." It means letting go of your ideas about "the way things should be" and yielding to the way things really are. It is submission to reality.

So your loved one is an alcoholic—that's a fact. Acceptance means you don't waste time and energy denying that or stewing about the unfairness of it all or indulging in escapist fantasies. In acceptance, you don't butt your head against a brick wall, demanding that another person be someone he's not. Let's face it, we believe most of life's problems would be solved easily if we could just change other people. But it doesn't work that way. We can influence others only by changing ourselves.

At the same time acceptance doesn't mean putting up with abuse or unacceptable behavior. Neither does it mean treating an alcoholic exactly like a nonalcoholic or writing off a drinker as someone who will never change. People do change, and sometimes it happens in response to our own changes.

Acceptance just recognizes that the behavior of other people is normal *for them*, given their own circumstances, personalities, and values. Getting drunk, for instance, is normal behavior for an alcoholic. So is arrogance. How angry can you get at normal behavior?

Then, too, anger is always at least partly directed toward God for allowing the conditions to exist that we find so unacceptable. When we accept that there is a purpose in whatever God allows, it should put things in perspective for us and help diminish our resentment. But that doesn't mean you should judge and condemn yourself for feeling angry. Instead, we are to accept ourselves as normal, human, and imperfect. Just remember that anger is a normal reaction, and anyone who lives with alcoholism usually has ample reason to get angry.

Then, too, you need acceptance in order to forgive and to love. Forgiveness is essential to your own happiness, and you can't forgive until your anger is neutralized. And you can only love others as they are, not as you wish they were. Authentic love doesn't demand that others devote themselves to making us happy. That's possessiveness, not love.

Acceptance is necessary for self-love, too. When you realize that no one exists for the express purpose of making you happy, you will take more responsibility for getting your own real needs met. If you are angry at your spouse for not spending time with you, for instance, you can fill some of those free evenings with a night-school class or good times with friends.

Anger or bitterness only helps keep you focused on and obsessed with your alcoholic, so it robs you of joy and peace. In this way you are giving the alcoholic enormous power to control your moods. It can be incredibly liberating to take back that power. When you say, "I have the right to be angry" you are really saying you have the right to be unhappy. And you do, but is that what you want?

Your Mind Is the Key

God's Word tells us, "Be made new in the attitude of your minds," and as part of this process, we are to "get rid of all bitterness, rage and anger, brawling and slander, along with every form of malice. Be kind and compassionate to one another, forgiving each other, just as in Christ God forgave you" (Eph. 4:23, 31–32).

From this we see that our emotions are under the control of our minds. We *can* "help it." No one really "makes" us angry; we make ourselves angry by our reactions to what happens. Here are some of the errors in our thinking that cause these faulty reactions:

1. *Labeling* others as "jerk," "idiot," "no-good," "stupid," or "creep." Let's face it, people aren't all good or all bad; they're just human like you and me. To label them is to assassinate their character and dismiss their value to God. Jesus had some pretty strong things to say on this subject. Read what he said in Matthew 5:21–22.

2. *Blaming*, or having to assign fault for everything that goes wrong. Some things are no one's fault. And sometimes it doesn't matter whose fault it is. People may be weak and imperfect but are often doing the best they can. Acceptance is better than blame. There are even times when we want to blame everything on alcoholism, but this just isn't realistic.

3. *Mind reading*. We invent motives for those who hurt us. We say, "He doesn't love me." "She doesn't think I'm important." These motives are strictly from our own imaginations. Just for the moment, pretend you are the person at whom you are angry and say, "Now why did I do what?" Try to see things from his or her point of view. It is even possible the other person's reactions had nothing to do with you. An alcoholic is seldom drinking *at you* and probably has no desire to hurt you.

4. *Exaggerating* the importance of some event that ticks you off. If your alcoholic loved one makes a crude joke in front of your church friends, remember the Al-Anon slogan "How important is it?" Few things are worth blowing your serenity.

"All-or-nothing thinking" is a form of gross exaggeration. When you hit a red light, you think, "I *always* get the red lights," but is that really true? And when you say to your drinker, "You're *never* around when I need you," you forget the times he or she has been.

5. *Maintaining unrealistic standards.* Most of us have a lot of rules for the way we think the world should function. And so often other people fail to live up to *our* high ideals. But is is important to accept the way things are. Husbands and wives are sometimes thoughtless and even cruel to each other. Babies don't always sleep the whole night through. When you catch yourself fussing and fuming about what should be, try to substitute the phrase, "It would be nice if . . ." You may find it helpful to write down your angry thoughts and consider them thoughtfully and prayerfully.

God's Word acknowledges that we all become angry from time to time, but it also reassures us that we can use our minds—at the point of our anger—to put out the flames. The often repeated injunction "Do not let the sun go down while you are angry," means that we are to deal with our anger as soon as we become aware of it. The writer of the book of James cautions us, "Everyone should be quick to listen, slow to speak and slow to become angry" (1:19). We are to remain cool and not jump to conclusions. An explosive temper tantrum harms both you and your victims.

Jesus said, "Anyone who is angry with his brother [some versions add "without cause"] will be subject to judgment" (Matt.5:22). It seems to me that the judgment will be invoked for the way the anger is handled rather than for the anger itself. Just as temper tantrums are wrong, so it is also wrong to deny anger and bottle it up until it becomes silent rage or hatred.

Finally, become aware of your anger. Accept it, and accept the person or situation that triggered it. Pray about it and talk it out with someone you can trust. Then forgive and forget. The wisdom writer called it right when he said, "A fool gives full vent to his anger, but a wise man keeps himself under control" (Prov. 29:11).

For Further Reflection

On anger, read Exodus 34:5–7; Proverbs 20:3; 22:24–25; 29:22; Matthew 5:21–26; 1 Corinthians 13:5; and James 1:19–21.

14 *More Kinds of Poison*

Hope deferred makes the heart sick, but a longing fulfilled is a tree of life.
PROVERBS 13:12

Have you been waiting and hoping for a long time for your loved one to stay sober without seeing any progress? Of this you can be sure—God understands that this can make you "sick at heart."

Anger is one very basic heartsick emotion that is directed outward toward those you hold responsible for your unhappiness. In this chapter we'll look at some other forms of heartsickness (or what I call poison) that are mostly directed inward. Acceptance helps neutralize these poisons the same way it does anger—acceptance of yourself and others just as you are.

Self-Pity

The "poor me" attitude of self-pity is the flip side of anger even though it is more passive than anger. This attitude is expressed in words such as, "Poor me; life just isn't fair and there's nothing I can do about it!"

My own tendency toward self-pity surfaced years before my anger. I suppose it helped me deny my anger for a time. It took Al-Anon to shake this attitude loose.

I went into an Al-Anon group thinking I would tell my sad story and they would pat me on the shoulder and say, "Poor Chris!" Imagine my surprise when they didn't, and when they told me instead that my life was in my own hands.

At one particular meeting, I was all upset because of a terrible scene at home that involved a struggle in the driveway over the car keys. I was crying and hardly noticed the plain-looking, thin woman on my right. Finally someone asked her how things were with her. "Oh, not bad," she replied. "I'm getting my feet back under me now, but it was rough when I returned from my mother's house a few weeks ago, after recovering there from my surgery. I'd told my husband I was coming, but there was no one to meet me at the airport. So I had to find another way home. When I got there, no one was at the apartment, but it was a terrible mess and all the furniture was gone. He had apparently moved in a half-a-dozen drinking buddies, and they'd sold all my family antiques for the money to buy more booze."

"Poor Chris" shrank to about two inches tall. I had not only a house full of furniture, but a husband who was a good provider and two lovely daughters. Thank you, dear friend, wherever you are, for teaching me that night to count my blessings.

Thankfulness is the main medicine for self-pity. God has given you your life, now and forever, as well as every good thing you have. Failure to appreciate it is an offense to him. But as the apostle Paul wrote, "Thanks be to God! He gives us the victory through our Lord Jesus Christ" (1 Cor. 15:57).

Envy

Envy is a close relative of anger and self-pity. To be envious means that we resent someone else who appears to be better off than we are. Like the other forms of nonacceptance, envy is a waste of precious time and energy, and it hurts you more than the person at whom you direct it.

Envy is similar to the other spiritual poisons in important ways. It is unloving (1 Cor. 13:4) and bad for the health, "A heart at peace gives life to the body, but envy rots the bones" (Prov. 14:30). Envy is based on unrealistic thoughts—if you think someone else's life seems ideal, you probably don't know that person well enough to be aware of his or her problems. After all, everyone has problems of one kind or another.

Sometimes we may also envy "sinners"—including the alcoholic—who seem to do whatever they want and get away with it. Feeling sorry for ourselves, we say, "God will forgive him when he gets around to asking, so why am I knocking myself out to do what's right?" Many of the psalms and proverbs in our Bible deal directly with this problem, and they assure us that the score will be settled someday. In Jesus' parable of the prodigal son, the older brother has this kind of envy (see Luke 15:11–32), but he shouldn't have. Even after his brother had returned and been forgiven, there were consequences for the young man: his share of the estate is still gone, and the older brother will inherit whatever is left.

The consequences of wrongdoing are inescapable no matter how much rescuing anyone does. And it isn't likely "their fun" is quite the way it appears to be.

Self-righteousness

The attitude that says, "I know it all and I'm always right, so I have the right to be angry at you" is self-righteousness, a form of pride. It, too, is based on a warped view of reality. None of us is that good, "for all have sinned and fall short of the glory of God" (Rom. 3:23).

It's easy for the close associate of an alcoholic to fall into this know-it-all trap, because you look so good by comparison. But it's not that black-and-white. In spite of what you may think, your alcoholic loved one is not wrong all the time about everything.

Actually, it may well be that your alcoholic uses your self-righteousness to justify bad behavior. Isn't that reason enough to stop pretending to be perfect?

We all need a healthy dose of humility. And that means knowing we need God, that we can't make it on our own. Just remember how often you have tried unsuccessfully to break a bad habit. Reflecting on your own failures will make you far less judgmental of someone else.

Lack of Forgiveness

If you are unable to forgive the alcoholic or others, it is likely you don't understand your position with God. Jesus said, "For if you forgive men when they sin against you, your heavenly Father will also forgive you. But if you do not forgive men their sins, your Father will not forgive your sins" (Matt. 6:14–15). That's a sobering thought, isn't it? God has much to forgive each one of us for, even if we are what the world calls a good person or a good Christian.

To forgive someone isn't to say that his or her sin was "all right," though. Forgiveness means you are willing to put it behind you, accept what happened, yield your anger, and not hold a grudge. It means you'll accept and love the person as if the offense never took place.

A wrong is still a wrong, though, and it's all right for the "guilty party" to take responsibility and accept the consequences. If a friend breaks something of yours, you can forgive her and still accept her offer to pay for it. In the same way, it's all right to allow an alcoholic to assume the consequences of his or her drinking.

Jesus said that if someone wrongs us and repents, we should be willing to forgive even seven times a day (Luke 17:3–6). And when the disciples said, "Increase our faith," it showed they understood the great emotional cost of such forgiveness. Let's face it—it is hard to give up our anger, because sometimes it feels so good. But the rewards are great: peace of mind and serenity.

But there's more. If it's hard to forgive someone who repents and asks forgiveness, what about someone who doesn't believe he has hurt you or doesn't care? It's harder to forgive that kind of person than someone who has expressed sorrow and regret, but you still need to do it for your own sake. May God increase *our* faith, too.

Guilt

Guilt is usually a real "biggie" for those who live with alcoholism. I'm not talking about genuine remorse for something we did that was wrong, which of course is constructive. Realistic remorse convicts you of sin while still allowing you to feel loved and forgiven by God when you ask forgiveness and make amends. No, what I'm referring to here is irrational or excessive guilt, which strikes at the very core of your being and makes you feel "rotten and just no good."

Irrational guilt makes you unable to forgive or accept yourself or believe that God forgives you. This is called condemnation, and there is nothing constructive about it. Condemnation is no more appropriate when directed toward yourself than toward anyone else. The apostle Paul reassured us when he wrote, "Therefore, there is now no condemnation for those who are in Christ Jesus" (Rom. 8:1).

Verbal abuse and rejection are the main reasons for excessive feelings of guilt and self-condemnation. If you were neglected, ignored, or made to feel worthless in early childhood, such feelings are deeply ingrained in your mind. An alcoholic will likely build on these feelings by heaping abuse on you as an adult. He or she may harp on all your real or imagined faults by saying, "Who wouldn't drink with a wife [husband, child, etc.] like you?" After a time that kind of abuse gets to you until you come to believe that you are worthless, even as you argue back and try to prove the drinker wrong. But the truth is that you are a precious and valuable person in God's eyes. And anyone who puts you down does so because of his or her own spiritual problems.

Then, too, errors in thinking also contribute to irrational feelings of guilt. First, we think we are supposed to be perfect: "I failed; therefore, I'm a bad person." Not at all! We all fail; you are a normal person. Deal with your failure and start over. Our errors in thinking have some of the same roots as those that cause fear and insecurity. We think we should be powerful enough to make the world right and to offset all the wrong choices made by others, including the drinker. But we have already seen what nonsense that idea is.

We also think that somehow we should be able to predict the future. How often we've said, "I should have known what was going to happen so I could have done something differently." However, not knowing all the results of our actions in advance is just something we have to accept.

Sometimes we also have the mistaken idea that we are obligated to undertake whatever anyone asks us to do. When someone decides you are the "perfect person" to take on a volunteer project that's really more than you can handle, do you feel guilty when you say no? Or do you say yes when you shouldn't? It is quite natural to want to be all things to all people, but we can't.

There are times when we say no angrily—especially to children—as a cover-up for this kind of guilt. But then we feel guilty for getting angry. So often we seem to be caught in a vicious cycle. It is important, though, to set priorities, and sometimes that means saying no to good things, not just bad things. In such cases, it's better for everyone when we turn down a request politely, without displaying inappropriate anger.

Approval seeking is another source of inappropriate guilt. In our struggle for approval we try to please everyone. We have a craving for praise and feel crushed if we are criticized. We allow ourselves to be overvulnerable to the opinions of others, believing that if a certain person disapproves of us he or she must be right.

Nonsense. People's opinions are naturally going to differ. You would be leading a very bland life if you never displeased anybody. When you receive criticism, stop and evaluate whether or not it is valid. And even if it is, concentrate on all the other things you did right that day.

Approval seeking may at times put a cruel twist on your relationship with your alcoholic loved one. It may well be that he registers strong approval for your rescuing behavior but then is bitterly critical when you refuse to take on his responsibilities. At such times you may end up feeling guilty for doing what is right. When that happens, just remember "it's the disease talking" and refuse to cater to or reinforce the alcoholic's behavior.

At times feelings of guilt come from lack of acceptance of our own negative feelings. Resentment of bad treatment builds up, and we may experience moments of wishing the alcoholic were dead and out of our life completely. But then we're flooded with remorse and berate ourselves. After all, we're convinced that only a bad person would harbor thoughts like that!

That's the time to accept your feelings and reaffirm that you are not a bad person. Then you won't need to get into rescuing and caretaking just to prove you are a loving person. Just remember when you are overwhelmed with that kind of guilt that love isn't warm, fuzzy feelings. Rather, it's concern for the highest good of the one you love.

Depression

Freud and other early psychoanalysts believed that depression is anger turned inward—that if you keep your anger inside long enough, you'll turn it against yourself. Some modern psychologists think lack of self-esteem is the major cause of depression. It seems to me that both opinions may be partly right—our guilt about our anger may reduce self-esteem until we don't like or trust ourselves enough to do anything constructive. At the same time depression can also be a symptom of various physical problems. Consequently the first thing a seriously depressed person should do is undergo a thorough medical checkup. This is discussed more fully in chapter 17.

Burnout—Time to Refuel

To live with alcoholism is to experience heavy spiritual warfare every day. It's no wonder that you become emotionally drained from time to time; the "poisons" take their toll and rob you of power. That is the time to recharge your "spiritual batteries."

Sometimes this means getting away for a while. Moses, Elijah, John the Baptist, even Jesus—all needed protracted times of solitude and communion with the Father. And they returned from their "desert times" with a fresh burst of power to help others. Maybe you can't escape for a long period of time, but possibly you could manage a weekend a few times a year for solitude, prayer, and rest.

Question: How can you know when you are "burned out" enough to need an extended period of rest and change? You will know for sure when you dip to the disorganized emotional level of your alcoholic loved one, when you are unable to remain detached, and when you can no longer keep your identity separate from the drinker's. You will know you need to get away when you are always worried or obsessed about something you can't change, when you are unable to concentrate on work or serious reading matter, when you live from hour to hour with no particular plan, and when you feel helpless and out of control. But please don't let things get that bad before you take time off for rest and change.

It's true that you may not be able to retreat to an exotic hideaway, but how about an off-season motel cabin, a tent in a quiet state park, or the home of a friend or relative? It's important, though, to be alone in fairly quiet surroundings and with few distractions. Above all, don't feel guilty about leaving your family; they'll survive if you make adequate arrangements, and you'll be better able to meet their needs because of your "break."

While you're away, get lots of rest. Take walks for exercise, read your Bible, and pray often. You may want to try fasting. Do things when you feel like it, and take advantage of the fact that you don't need to keep to a schedule. Be introspective; record your thoughts and feelings in a journal.

Your "poisons" may come to the surface and make you unhappy for a time, but that's because you are getting rid of them. The benefits come later. You'll gain some perspective, and when you're back home, you'll be able to see changes that need to be made. Remember, you are only a "pipeline" for God's love and power; your rest and relaxation time should open your pipeline so that you are better able to give and receive that love.

By changing your way of thinking, you can help prevent poisonous negative emotions from blocking your way to a better life. It will be necessary to develop a certain amount of detachment from your own thoughts, and that is a tricky process. But you'll do well to ask yourself, "Does it make sense to think the way I always have, or is there a better way?" Then as you spend time in God's Word, you'll receive help in putting it all together. And by practicing tough love, you'll give your alcoholic the best chance to get well, and you will have the peace of mind you need so much. The psalmist understood the rewards of being quiet and alone when he wrote, "The Lord is my shepherd, I shall lack nothing. He makes me lie down in green pastures, he leads me beside quiet waters, he restores my soul" (Ps. 23:1–3).

For Further Reflection

On thankfulness versus self-pity, read Psalm 100; Philippians 4:11–13; 1 Thessalonians 5:16–18; and Hebrews 12:28.

On envy, read Psalm 37 and James 3:13–18.

On self-righteousness, read Proverbs 14:12; 15:31–33; 18:17; Romans 3:21–27; 7:15–8:4; 12:3 and 1 John 1:8–10.

On forgiveness, read Psalms 19:12–14; 32; 51; Matthew 6:12–15; 18:21–35; Mark 11:25; and Luke 7:36–50.

On guilt, read Psalm 130:3–4; Isaiah 43:25; John 3:16–18; Romans 8:1–2; Galatians 1:10; Hebrews 10:22; and 1 John 3:18–24.

Part 5 Through Domestic
Misery to a Peaceful
Home

15 *Defuse Those Arguments*

> Consider what a great forest is set on fire by a small spark. The tongue also is a fire, a world of evil among the parts of the body. It corrupts the whole person, sets the whole course of his life on fire, and is itself set on fire by hell. . . . With the tongue we praise our Lord and Father, and with it we curse men, who have been made in God's likeness. Out of the same mouth come praise and cursing. My brothers, this should not be.
>
> JAMES 3:5b–6, 9–10

Arguments have to be one of the worst things that happen when you live with an alcohol abuser. The loud, ugly quarrels that shake many of our homes are destructive to the human spirit. They are not proper confrontations (which are limited, controlled, and should be motivated by love) but attempts at confrontation that get out of control and are motivated by anger and spite. Arguments drive wedges between family members, seldom settle any issue, and ruin the peace of the home. No one "wins" an argument!

If there are children in the home, arguments between their parents hurt them worst of all. Whether they are little ones or teenagers, family quarrels destroy their sense of security. And, tragically, the children often blame themselves for problems that have nothing to do with them.

Does It Take Two to Quarrel?

Who starts the arguments in your home? Is it necessarily the one doing all the yelling? Or is it the one who provokes the other with reproving glances, sarcastic jokes, sulky silences, or neglects responsibilities? And once an argument starts, do you feel compelled to help keep it going?

By all means, avoid starting arguments even though your spouse seems to be begging for a fight. (I'm assuming for this chapter that your alcoholic is your marriage partner; if not, maybe there's still something here that you can use.)

If your husband, for example, is intoxicated, he may be very belligerent and uncivil. Everything that goes wrong is your fault, and nothing you say is right. He criticizes anything and everything about you—your housekeeping or home maintenance, cooking, parenting skills, religion, occupation, looks, and family. Eventually comes a shouting match that continues until bedtime, when you both withdraw into a stony silence.

The main reason an alcoholic wants an argument comes under the heading of "projection"—the psychological process by which a person with a crushing load of guilt and self-hatred tries to unload it on someone else by turning it outward as anger. The alcoholic dumps his or her self-loathing on you because you are close and handy. It has nothing to do with your own worth as a person. I once heard an Al-Anon member say, "If Florence Nightingale had been married to an alcoholic, he would have told her she was a lousy nurse."

Once you understand "projection," it should help you not to carry around so much irrational guilt. Just remember that when he lays a guilt trip on you, it's his own guilt talking. At the same time you should also understand why the drinker cuts down your efforts at self-improvement. If you are a wife, you may be baffled and hurt when you spend an entire week cleaning the house in response to your husband's complaints, and then he rants and raves about a curtain that is not quite straight. Just know that he just needs something to complain about, and he'll find it.

Another reason your alcoholic wants to pick a fight is so you can take on the role of the "heavy." If your alcoholic wife can get you to yell at her, she can experience your anger as a punishment or penance, relieving her of any guilt she feels about drinking.

Frontline Maneuvers

Now we agree that a quarrel is a good thing to avoid. And under-standing the alcoholic's motives will help you not take the insults so personally, so that your reaction need not be so strong or obvious. Here are some other "frontline maneuvers" that will help you either avoid arguments or lessen their severity:

1. Be good to yourself on a daily basis. It's harder to pick a fight with a happy person. Whatever is good for you is good for the alcoholic.

2. Pray every day that you'll both have a good day and for strength and wisdom in any tricky situation.

3. Learn your alcoholic's "language of love" (see chapter 12) so that you'll know you are doing loving things for him or her and you'll be less vulnerable to guilt. Build up the alcoholic with praise and a big smile when he or she does something that pleases you, no matter how simple a thing it is.

4. Save confrontations for morning. Things are more likely to get out of hand around suppertime and after, when most of us are physically at a low ebb (and when a drinker has more alcohol in the system).

5. Keep working on detachment and acceptance. It would help to use a copy of *One Day at a Time in Al-Anon*, which you can get at a meeting of your local group. Be patient with yourself. Lifetime attitudes and habits aren't going to be reversed overnight.

6. Remember that it's projection when verbal abuse starts. If you keep in mind that it's really the alcoholic's self-hatred talking, you can't help but feel compassion. Don't let your self-esteem be dragged down; you don't deserve bad treatment just because you're getting it.

7. See the humor in it. This calls for a lot of detachment, but the alcoholic's efforts to provoke you by jumping from one ridiculous insult to another can actually be amusing, if you pay attention to what he's doing instead of what he says.

8. Keep your own voice down. Our tendency is to shout when shouted at. If you stick with a quiet answer, the other person may

have to turn down his or her own volume to hear you. Your tone of voice should be calm and gentle. If someone were to tape your discussion, how would *you* sound?

9. Give a vague answer when you need to give one at all. Say something like, "Oh, is that how you see it?" It's better to say something neutral than to keep up a hostile silence. "A gentle answer turns away wrath, but a harsh word stirs up anger" (Prov. 15:1).

10. Don't set the alcoholic off by saying, "You've been drinking again." She knows it and she knows you know it. Don't be furious about denial; denial is normal, remember?

11. React as little as possible when insulted. If you cry, shout, defend yourself, or make counteraccusations when verbally abused, the alcoholic will experience that as a reward: "It worked!" And you'll be sure to hear the same thing the next time. "A fool shows his annoyance at once, but a prudent man overlooks an insult" (Prov. 12:16).

12. Change the subject. A drunk is almost as distractable as a two-year-old, so use this fact to your advantage. When he gets onto a subject that really bothers you, ask him about something else. For example, "Here's an article on the new Chryslers. Do you like the styling?" Do this as many times as you have to, using different topics. He may not calm down, but he may become distracted and switch to another subject.

13. Music hath charms. In the Bible story David used music to soothe the often irrational King Saul. It is useful both in preventing arguments and in distraction. Any kind of good, wholesome music your alcoholic likes will do, whether you play it on the stereo or sing or play an instrument yourself.

14. Listen and agree when possible. It's okay to "tune out" someone who is being verbally abusive. But if you happen to catch what sounds like a reasonable idea, agree with it. It will take the wind out of his sails if he expects automatic opposition. Make sure you understand by repeating back the good idea, "So you think it makes more sense to get a new furnace than to spend the money on repairs?"

15. Don't preach. Witnessing, hymn singing, and Scripture quot-

ing, when done in excess to an angry person, will do more harm than good. A little goes a long way. As a friend of mine once said, "Let the Holy Spirit do the convicting." If you are asked questions about spiritual matters, ask the Holy Spirit to give you the right reply. Otherwise, easy does it. Your attitude is a better witness than your words most of the time.

Sexual Fulfillment in Marriage

Sexuality in marriage is meant to be a natural, beautiful gift from God (see 1 Cor. 7:1-7). Spouses are not to deprive each other under normal circumstances. I have read one well-meaning author who says a husband or wife has a "duty to refuse" sex to a spouse who has been drinking. I feel this is an unfair burden. For one thing, you don't always know for sure when your spouse has been drinking, or how much. For another, if you want to make love and can get some pleasure from it, why should you be deprived? You have enough people wanting to take various choices out of your hands without taking away that one, too. It's not your obligation to use sex as a system of reward and punishment for your spouse.

On the other hand, you may, understandably, want to avoid sex on an occasion when drunkenness has "turned you off." A person under the influence of liquor may not be clean and may smell like alcohol or may use bad language and be verbally abusive. At such times a man may become unable to maintain an erection or may continue intercourse too long without being able to climax. Neither a husband nor wife is obligated under Scripture, I firmly believe, to submit under such degrading conditions.

"Creative avoidance" is the concept to keep in mind when you want to avoid sex. Find a tactful way to say "not right now," and your spouse will understand that you don't mean "not ever." "Let's wait till morning," or "How about tomorrow night?" will meet with less resistance than a plain no. Long baths and similar delaying tactics, until the spouse goes to sleep, can be useful too. Moment by moment, the choice is yours.

Finances

Money is a frequent topic for arguments in any family. But alcohol abuse poses additional problems as money is wasted on liquor and mismanaged in other ways. Although this is controversial, I think the spouse of an alcoholic is justified in keeping his or her money separate from that of the drinking spouse if that will avoid bankruptcy. In extreme cases, legal separations have been obtained for this reason. These are not normally good things to do. Ideally, a husband and wife should act as a team in setting their financial goals and sticking to them. However when this doesn't work, it becomes one more tragic consequence of drunkenness.

Here are some bare-bones principles from Scripture on finances: Trust in the Lord for all your real needs and he will provide. Keep your needs simple. Be thrifty. Don't get into debt. Ideally the husband is the leader, but either spouse can be the bookkeeper. It is a sin to refuse to provide for one's family. Work hard and practice sound management. A home-based craft or business could be ideal for a mother who wants to be with her children, as in Proverbs 31:10–31.

Above all, don't be secretive about finances. Both partners should be fully aware of all bank accounts, debts, investments, insurance policies, and so on. Study carefully the biblical references listed at the end of this chapter. In addition you may find help from a good Christian book on family finances.

It is important to remember, though, that many arguments can be avoided or reduced in severity when you keep your attitudes in line, and a "soft answer" will help to cool off anger. The apostle Paul gave us some good advice when he wrote, "Do not let any unwholesome talk come out of your mouths, but only what is helpful for building others up according to their needs, that it may benefit those who listen" (Eph. 4:29).

For Further Reflection

On arguments, read Proverbs 10:11, 19; 12:18; 13:3; 17:1, 19; 18:13; 19:11; 20:22; 26:2, 4.

On finances, read Psalm 37; Proverbs 13:11; 15:16–17; 16:16; 21:17; 23:4–8; 30:8–9; 31:10–31; Ecclesiastes 4:6; Matthew 25:14–30; Luke 9:10–17; 12:13–34; 2 Corinthians 9:6–7; Colossians 3:23–24; 1 Thessalonians 4:11–12; 2 Thessalonians 3:10–13; and 1 Timothy 5:8

16 *Abuse: It's Not All Right*

If an enemy were insulting me, I could endure it;
if a foe were raising himself against me,
    I could hide from him.
But it is you, a man like myself,
    my companion, my close friend,
with whom I once enjoyed sweet fellowship.   PSALM 55:12–14

To "abuse" is to use wrongly, treat improperly, or violate. It really is a terrible emotional injury to be turned against by someone you love and trust—someone you thought would love you for a lifetime. As Shakespeare's Marc Antony said, it is "the most unkindest cut of all."

Types of Abuse

There are four main classifications of abuse. *Verbal abuse*, as discussed in the last chapter, includes insults and put-downs designed to hurt another person and destroy self-esteem. Put-downs may also be falsely attributed to a third party, as in "So-and-so said this about you." In this case, the purpose is also to drive a wedge between the victim and the third person.

Emotional abuse covers all other kinds of attempts to hurt mentally and emotionally. These sick mind games can include the following:

- Punishing you with prolonged silences.
- Arrogance—he is always right, and his opinion is the only one that matters.
- The King Tut syndrome—his accomplishments are wonderful; yours are meaningless. He implies that he does you a favor by continuing to put up with you.

- Playing "you're the crazy one." He denies the truth of various things you saw or heard for yourself, even when he knows them to be true. "Your imagination is playing tricks on you again, dear."
- Acting like Prince Charming in public and King Tut in private.
- Ignoring you completely in public, refusing to hear your questions or even leaving without telling you.
- Openly flirting with other people of the opposite sex, open admiration of others' physical attributes, implying that they are more attractive than you.

However, don't think for a minute alcoholics believe all this "garbage." They don't. They're like insecure preschoolers trying to puff up their own egos at someone else's expense. Even though such behavior hurts, don't "reward" it with a strong emotional reaction.

Intimidation is the use of force or threats to get one's own way—the use of fear to motivate another. It often starts with "house abuse"— holes punched through walls and so on. You are being intimidated when the alcoholic physically blocks you from leaving the house, disables your car, or threatens to injure or kill you if you step out of line. The lights may be turned off when you are trying to read or turned on when you are trying to sleep. Blankets may be pulled off the bed while you are in it, or dishes of food swept onto the floor. Intimidation includes any action meant to control you through the use of force, threats, or fear.

Physical abuse usually follows closely on the heels of intimidation. It starts in milder ways—not that any of it can be called "mild"—such as shoving the victim around or poking a finger into her chest to emphasize a point. (I say "her" because as a rule most victims of domestic violence are women. But it is equally damaging when a wife resorts to any form of physical abuse.)

Physical abuse can eventually include slapping, burning, kicking, punching, beating, and sometimes even rape. In extreme cases it ends in death by strangulation, head or internal injuries, shooting, or stabbing. And occasionally, the chronic abuser is killed by an abused spouse who finally "reaches the end of her rope."

Physical abuse is progressive. It usually gets worse if allowed to continue. And of one thing you can be sure: It doesn't get better unless action is taken to break the cycle. However, repentance and apologies are not "action."

Denial of physical abuse runs very, very deep in both the abuser and the one abused. The abuser may be horrified the day after an incident and promise it will never happen again. The victim wants to believe it. She can't bring herself to "punish him by leaving or getting professional help just when he is being so nice." Denial says, "It was just this one time. Things will get better now. I have to give him one more chance." This simply means that things are better for a while until they get worse again.

Causes of Abuse

Most domestic violence is connected with drug or alcohol abuse. Some of it is related to family traditions—many abusers of spouse or children were abused as children themselves or saw violence between their parents. Low self-esteem is a factor.

In writing to the Christians in Ephesus the apostle Paul said, "Husbands ought to love their wives as their own bodies. He who loves his wife loves himself" (Eph. 5:28). But the self-destructive use of alcohol and other drugs shows contempt for one's own body. And this self-hatred is just extended to the spouse's body in physical abuse.

The possibility of spiritual or demonic involvement in abuse should not be automatically ruled out, especially if the abuser's personality, voice, and facial expression are totally different than at other times. I think we Christians have sometimes been too blind to these influences. A friend of mine had firsthand experience with this problem. She found that when her husband was under satanic influence, she could control his behavior through the use of God's name. She could say, "In the name of Jesus Christ the Lord, sit down!" when he was threatening her, and he would do it for a short time. Pleading the blood of Jesus in prayer and quoting Scripture are effective weapons in such spiritual warfare.

If there is any question in your mind as to whether you are dealing with a demon, try doing what I have just suggested. If it makes a difference, you probably are—a person who is merely drunk or mentally ill would have no fearful reaction to the Word of God or your prayers. And if you have reason to suspect the worst, get some help from those in your Christian community who are experienced in dealing with such things. My friend did, much to her relief.

What to Do If You Are Abused

If you are suffering abuse, particularly physical abuse or intimidation, there are two things to do right away that are both important. First, ask for God's help and protection, and then seek out whatever human help is available to you. Asking for God's help is serious business and will make a difference, but it doesn't rule out accepting human help. The wisdom writer gave us good advice, "The prudent see danger and take refuge, but the simple keep going and suffer for it" (Prov. 27:12). "Taking refuge" doesn't mean you are weak or don't trust God. Don't let a bad situation continue just because of pride.

Many cities now have shelters for battered women and their children. You can find their phone numbers on public bulletin boards or in the telephone book. There is no shame in using such services. They exist because people really want to help. You may also have friends, especially in your church family, who would love to open their homes to you if they knew you had a need. Talk to a close friend or to your pastor. You may feel in a desperate moment, "There's no way I could disturb a family in the middle of the night." But some people would count it a privilege to help you. Give them a chance.

It is also appropriate to call the police and to file charges in a case of physical abuse. Unfortunately, many police agencies have in the past taken too casual an attitude toward domestic violence and have often refused to do more than give the abuser a warning. But this attitude is somewhat understandable, because many victims file charges and then drop them the next day. If you take such an action, follow through. Recent studies have shown that legal action can help deter further abuse, and many police departments are becoming more responsive to victims of abuse.

It is true that Jesus said on one occasion, "If someone strikes you on one cheek, turn to him the other also" (Luke 6:29). But he was speaking there about suffering religious persecution as Christians. Spouse abuse is a different situation. It is not a bad thing—some would call it a civic duty—to report a crime against you, and that's what assault is.

Once you have dealt with the immediate emergency, you should take steps to get some pastoral or professional counseling. In this way you can gain perspective and rebuild your self-esteem. This is still important even if the abuse is "merely" verbal and emotional. To endure abuse of any kind is to be battered in mind, soul, and spirit, and "a crushed spirit who can bear?" (Prov. 18:14).

The Submission Question

In writing to the Colossian Christians, Paul said, "Wives, submit to your husbands, as is fitting in the Lord" (Col. 3:18). This concept of submission in marriage is difficult for almost everyone these days. And it is even more so when the husband is frequently drunk, irrational, and/or abusive! Frequently, an abused wife hears submission taught in a very strict way in her church. Sometimes the pastor does indicate there are exceptions—a woman shouldn't rob a bank if her husband tells her to. But he seldom says what to do if the husband is drunk, drugged, out of his mind, or violent. A wife can become confused. "If he tells me to jump off a bridge, am I supposed to do that?" she wonders. It's no rhetorical question. Wives are asked every day to do things that make about as much sense as jumping off a bridge.

The concept of submission is still valid today, but it is widely misunderstood and often wrongly preached. Submission isn't blind obedience, and it isn't being a doormat. It is a creative act that calls for intelligence, diplomacy, tact, and wisdom. If a wife is to submit "as is fitting in the Lord," then obviously that cannot include morally wrong or senseless acts that the Lord would not consider "fitting." Virtually everyone agrees that you shouldn't submit when it means doing something morally wrong. But what about requests that are just stupid or pointless?

Len was embarrassed one night when Marilyn insisted on driving home from a fair because he was drunk. Two weeks later, drunk again and still enraged about the incident, he demanded that she get into the car with him, return to the fairgrounds, and apologize to the parking lot attendants. Never mind that the fair was over, and no one was there anymore. Never mind that three sleeping children would be left alone in the house. Marilyn refused, but secretly wondered if she were disobeying God by not doing what her husband wanted. I think it could hardly have been "fitting in the Lord" for her to go. She would have been submitting to craziness and sickness, not to her husband's true self or his best interests.

At the same time a husband has obligations that go hand in hand with wifely submission. He is to provide sane, loving leadership (see I Pet. 3:7; Eph. 5:28–29, and Col. 3:19). Each partner's ability to be faithful to the scriptural ideal depends upon the other's obedience. A wife cannot be totally submissive to a husband who isn't providing godly leadership. Neither can a husband lead lovingly if his wife is selfish and rebellious.

When one spouse is being overcompliant and the other is taking advantage through selfish domination, the result is an unhealthy, out-of-balance relationship. The marriage becomes a sick power trip in which neither partner really respects the other. To submit to such destructiveness is not really a loving act. Rather, it is an implied agreeement with your domineering spouse's low opinion of both of you. I really think it's more loving for the dominated partner— husband or wife—to take a strong stand. In doing this, you are saying, "I respect both of us enough to want a better way of life for us."

At the same time, either a husband or wife can show love by letting the spouse have his or her way when the issue has nothing to do with right, wrong, or alcoholism. If you voluntarily give up "having it your way" with a smile on minor issues, your spouse can't say, "You're against me on everything." It is wise to save your strength and newfound firmness for times when you'll really need them.

At all times your primary purpose should be to do the will of God, not to prove anything to your spouse. Nevertheless, your loving, Christ-like example will speak louder than words. Your example will mean more to your spouse and others than you will ever know.

Drunk Driving—a Good Starting Point

If you are looking for a good place to draw a line in refusing to submit to the disease of alcoholism, here's a great place—don't tolerate drunken driving. It's a form of abuse in itself. Don't ride with any drunk driver, ever, and don't permit your minor children to do so.

If there are alcoholics among your relatives and close friends, the people around you are going to think you're being unreasonable in taking your stand. Yes, it will be a hassle. You may have to decline some invitations that you know will end with this possibility. You may have to find another ride or stay somewhere overnight when you weren't planning to. You may even have to refuse to let little David go to the races with his uncle if the uncle is likely to drink while there. You may even have to say to your wife or husband, "If you leave now with that child, I'll call the police as soon as you're gone."

Not three miles from where I live, a car left the road and turned over in a flooded irrigation ditch. The young couple escaped without injury, but their little son was killed. The father was charged with driving while intoxicated. The mother wasn't charged with anything but she will have to live out her life knowing she could have prevented this accident.

What can you do, or should you do, when you know the alcoholic is driving drunk while alone? Innocent people are on the road, and their lives are endangered along with your loved one's. Surely it is fruitless to argue about it, but some people have resorted to "losing" the car keys. Or, if it is too late for that, you might consider reporting the intoxicated driver to the police—if you are very sure about the intoxication.

Can a Christian Separate?

In extreme cases, the only way for an abused spouse to achieve any kind of peace and safety is to live apart for a time. Often, nothing else will convince the abuser that the abuse must stop. Therefore, the question of marital separation must be discussed in this context.

The true remedies for abuse—increased self-esteem, personal growth, and better communication—all take time. In the beginning, such improvements feel like throwing buckets of water into a forest fire. The fire still rages out of control, and someone could get burned—perhaps fatally.

Separation, for a Bible-believing Christian, is quite different from divorce. Secular society assumes that any separation is going to be permanent, and that divorce is merely the legal technicality that makes it final. But the serious Christian reads in the Bible that "a wife must not separate from her husband. But if she does, she must remain unmarried or else be reconciled to her husband. And a husband must not divorce his wife" (1 Cor. 7:10b–11). And Jesus himself said, "Therefore what God has joined together, let man not separate" (Matt. 19:6b).

Consider the words "but if she does" in 1 Corinthians 7. Does the Bible ever speak that way about sin or completely forbidden conduct? The following words tell the right way to separate, implying that separation, while not normally a good idea, may sometimes be necessary. Can you imagine a commandment that says, "Thou shalt not steal—but if you do, here's the right way to do it"?

Christian separation, as I see it, is meant to be temporary—it's like what doctors do when they rebreak and set a broken leg that is healing wrong. It's painful, but in some cases it needs to be done if the patient is ever to walk properly again.

I am not convinced that there is ever a good reason for a Christian to seek a divorce. (Some Christian teachers allow it if the cause is habitual adultery.) I believe that if a Christian leaves a spouse because of drunkenness or abuse, it should be with the intention to remain sexually faithful and with the hope of reconciliation through sobriety. It is reasonable to insist on a good treatment program, and perhaps marriage counseling, as a condition of getting back together.

If your spouse should leave you, the apostle Paul makes it clear that it's all right to let him or her go without a struggle (1 Cor. 7:12-16). (Many Christians believe that this passage conveys the right to remarry in such a case.)

If you don't want a divorce, say so, but don't put up an elaborate resistance. It may be your pride that is hurt more than anything else. When an alcoholic rejects you, it's usually because you are too much of a threat to the disease. It doesn't have anything to do with your attractiveness or desirability as a partner. Just keep working on your own personal growth; otherwise, you could fall into another, similar relationship in spite of your best intentions.

Next, comes the question, How bad must things be before you consider separation? Only you can decide that. No one knows better than you how deeply you have been affected by abuse, or how much you can take and still function well. But spend much time in prayer before making such a decision. And, ignore the unasked-for advice you will get. The people who say "throw the bum out" are not going to be around when you are broke, lonely, and in need of help. The people who are "shocked that you could think of leaving" haven't lived with abuse. (Many Christians, even pastors, have been sheltered from such problems and are pretty naive about abuse.) Watch your ultimatums, though, and don't threaten to leave unless you are planning to follow through.

If you do leave, make sure your spouse knows that you are planning to be faithful—that you have left the house but not the marriage. Be clear about what your conditions are for a reconciliation. A lawyer may be a help in working out financial and child custody arrangements—a Christian lawyer may be more likely to understand your goals.

Be sure to maintain your detachment during the separation. Don't be constantly checking up on your spouse's condition. If your spouse starts dating, you'll have to be prepared to deal with that. Get some counseling, but don't allow anyone to make your decisions for you. Enjoy your freedom and the relative peace and quiet, and if your life seems too empty now, fill the spaces with a new hobby or career skill. If possible, live on your own, not with relatives—you need to be an adult and stand on your own feet. Beware of friendships with someone of the opposite sex: don't lead yourself into temptation.

The bottom line is simply this—you don't have to endure abuse forever, and you aren't being particularly spiritual or loving if you do. Breaking the cycle of abuse may turn out to be the most loving thing you ever do. Ask God to show you the best way for you to break that cycle. It won't be easy, but it is possible and it must be done.

The psalmist spoke to our need when he wrote,

> I cry to you, O Lord;
>   I say, "You are my refuge,
>   my portion in the land of the living.
> Listen to my cry,
>   for I am in desperate need;
> rescue me from those who pursue me,
>   for they are too strong for me.
> Set me free from my prison,
>   that I may praise your name (Ps. 142:5–7).

For Further Reflection

On calling upon God for help, read Psalms 18; 20; 22; 55; 56; 142; 143; and others.

On marriage and divorce, read Proverbs 14:1; Matthew 5:27–32; 19:3–12; Romans 7:1–4; 1 Corinthians 7:10–40; Ephesians 5:22–33; and 1 Peter 3:1–7.

On decision making, read Proverbs 2:1–15; 16; 19:21; 21:30–31.

Part 6   Through Martyrdom to a Healthy Self-love

17 *Self-esteem Is Not Selfishness*

"Love the Lord your God with all your heart and with all your soul and with all your mind." This is the first and greatest commandment. And the second is like it: "Love your neighbor as yourself." All the Law and the Prophets hang on these two commandments.   MATTHEW 22:37–40

Did you ever stop to think about what this Scripture actually says? Sometimes we overinterpret it and think it says, "Love your neighbor *instead of* yourself." But no—it says to love God first and then your neighbor *as* yourself. Jesus assumes here that we have a natural love for ourselves that we can use as a reference point in loving others. If you don't love yourself, how will you know how to love anyone else? Jesus also says, "In everything, do to others what you would have them do to you" (Matt. 7:12). If you had no ideas about how others should treat you with decency and respect, you wouldn't know how to treat them. So a certain amount of self-love is not only okay, it's a necessity in forming positive relationships with others.

We are all born with the capacity for self-love and only gradually learn how to love others. A baby cries when hungry, uncomfortable, or lonely—never knowing or caring that Mommy is tired or has other things to do. If the baby receives lots of good, loving care, eventually a spark of love is born in him or her and begins to turn outward.

But what happens if no one expresses an adequate amount of love and care for the baby? In such cases, children learn not to trust or depend on anyone else very much. They also think they aren't worth much, if no one hugs or kisses them or says loving things to them. They might learn to meet the needs of others, but they'll be motivated by a need for scraps of approval or the desire to avoid punishment and mistreatment—not by love for its own sake.

131

The child that is cuddled and cared for has an adequate amount of self-esteem. He or she isn't afraid to "run out of love" because there seems to be a steady supply of it around. This child is secure. The child that doesn't receive love and care has little self-esteem, does not feel lovable, and is afraid to trust anyone too much. This little one is insecure. These are extremes, of course, and many of us fall somewhere between the two.

As we read our Bible, especially Psalms and the Gospels, we get an idea of how important we are to God. It can be hard to understand, if no human being has ever modeled that love to you generously and unconditionally. But Jesus loved you enough to die for you. So when you respect your own worth as a person, you are just agreeing with him.

Question: How is self-esteem lost or damaged? We have seen how early childhood experiences are crucial, as the treatment we receive from others continues to be important in adulthood. Unfortunately, in our Western society, we tend to base self-esteem too much on the work we do. Work is good, of course, but our value to God is the same whether we have a high-paying job, a low-paying job, or a nonpaying job such as that of a mother at home. And it is sad, but many people let their self-esteem be destroyed if they are fired or laid off or when they retire or become disabled.

It is significant that marriage to an alcoholic goes hand in hand with low self-esteem. If our opinion of ourselves is low, we are more likely to choose as a partner someone like an alcoholic—a person wrapped up in himself who will probably not treat us very well. Besides, we aren't sure we deserve good treatment anyway.

Our own negative thought patterns, long established, work against self-esteem. We tell ourselves things like these:

> I always fail.
> The good things I do don't count; anyone could do them.
> Whatever goes wrong, it's my fault.
> Nobody loves me; but then, why should they?
> Other people are smarter or better than I am.
> If someone puts me down, he or she must be right.
> No matter what I try to do, it won't work.

We need to counter negative thoughts with positive ones:

God loves me, so there must be something there to love.

Some people like and respect me.

Some of the things I do turn out well.

I have certain gifts and talents.

If I make a mistake sometimes, I'm only human and I'll learn from it.

I'm not always to blame, and others don't always know more than I do.

I am smart and talented and strong enough to succeed with God's help.

Write down your favorite positive thoughts on index cards and keep them where you'll see them often. Include Bible verses such as "I can do everything through him who gives me strength" (Phil. 4:13).

Don't Do Jesus' Job for Him

Negative thinking and irrational guilt lead to false martyrdom. A real Christian martyr is someone who suffers religious persecution and stands up to it well. That isn't what a false martyr does. A false martyr thinks, "It's my job—or it seems to be my fate—to suffer for everyone else and be unhappy so they can be happy." A false martyr bases his or her whole identity on suffering and would hardly know what to do without it. The false martyr is attempting to atone for sin—his own or others'—through suffering. This shows a lack of acceptance for what Jesus did for us on the cross, "For Christ died for sins once for all" (1 Pet. 3:18), and there is nothing you or I can do to "help out" the Lord in this way.

False martyrdom has little to do with love, for it makes the "martyr" angry and bitter eventually when the loved ones for whom he or she has "given up everything" fail to appreciate the sacrifice. If poor self-esteem has led you into this trap, *you can and should give it up*. It only leads to actions that prolong alcoholism and keeps family relationships unhealthy. Don't try to be someone's "savior." There's only one qualified for the job, and it isn't you.

Overcome Depression

Depression is another possible result of a lack of self-esteem, although depression can have other causes, including physical illness or a disturbance in body chemistry.

Low self-esteem and negative thinking lead to depression when we learn to feel helpless and when we no longer believe we have the power to do anything right or change anything for the better. If "nothing I do makes any difference," then sooner or later I'm going to give up trying to do anything. I'll mope around in my bathrobe, emotionally paralyzed. The things I should be doing will seem impossibly difficult.

Fortunately for me personally, when I have a spell like this, it usually lasts only an hour or two. For some, it can go on for days, weeks, or months. Unfortunately, the only way to get out of it is to "pull yourself up by your own socks." There are things you can do to help yourself at home when depression strikes. It is important at such times to *do something constructive*, no matter what, no matter how small. If a job seems too large to tackle, break it down into bite-size steps and just take one bite. If your paperwork is out of control, for instance, just tell yourself you'll sit down at the desk for five minutes, open one envelope, and read what's inside. (You may end up doing more, of course, but after you've fulfilled your "agreement" you can quit anytime you like.)

When "one day at a time" is too much, just take one hour or a few minutes at a time. I'm not a morning person at all. Sometimes I don't think I can stand up and go take a shower in the morning. So I tell myself, "I'll just get out some clean clothes and take them to the bathroom, that's all." Of course, once I get moving I don't mind taking a shower. The key is to think in terms of, "I can't do everything, but I can do something. Here is what I *can* do."

As Erma Bombeck once said: Know thyself. Then trick thyself.

It also helps lift depression when you get out of your rut and do something different. If a trip is too much, then go for a walk or take a different route to work or the store. If these things are too much, then at least vary things by sitting in a different chair. Anything to give yourself, literally, a different perspective.

Learn to Love Yourself

If your self-esteem isn't what it should be, you can work at improving it. Here are some specific things you can do to build up your self-esteem.

1. Praise yourself. Everyone needs to be told what they are doing right. Give yourself a verbal pat on the back when you deserve it: "You sure got a lot of work done today, Sue. Great job!" "You look nice in that new outfit, Fran." You may feel silly doing this; do it anyway.

2. React positively to criticism. Don't let criticism trigger your own negative thoughts. When someone criticizes you, make certain you fully understand what your critic is saying. Then decide whether the criticism is valid. If it is, discuss how you can change or improve your performance, without putting yourself down as a person. If it isn't, you can say, "I don't agree with what you are saying. Would you like to know why I did what I did?"

3. Forgive yourself. A good parent forgives you, and so does God when you confess your wrongs. If you have confessed your wrongs and made amends for them but are still torturing yourself over something that happened long ago, that's condemnation, and it's from Satan! Let it go and forgive yourself aloud. Put your past failures in perspective—you are human; life goes on; you must go on from where you are now.

4. Give yourself little gifts. Do you ever buy or make something nice for yourself "just because"? A new item of clothing, an ounce of cologne, an interesting book, or your own favorite dish for supper can give you a real lift. I'll bet you do nice things for the other people you love. Why not do them for yourself, too?

5. Take some time off. Do you feel worthwhile only when you're working? You wouldn't wish a life of constant drudgery on anyone else. An occasional hour, or even a whole day, to do exactly what you want—or nothing—is good medicine.

6. Look your best. When you look better, you feel better. It doesn't matter where you are going or who's going to see you. An attractive haircut is important. So is cleanliness, and so are clothes that flatter you and make you feel good.

7. Be around positive, supportive people. Have you ever noticed that certain people tend to build you up emotionally and spiritually when you are around them? Try to spend more time with them, and less time with anyone who makes you feel worse about yourself. Don't let your alcoholic cut you off from positive people in an effort to isolate you.

8. Build up others. Notice what it is your positive people do for you, and do it for others. Talk positively—listen to their problems neutrally, without promoting self-pity or giving unwanted advice. Admire and appreciate their good points—people are starving for an honest compliment! Doing this will make you feel better, too.

9. Exercise. Aerobic exercise releases chemicals in your brain that actually improve your mood. Walking is especially good because you can do it almost anywhere, and because a change of scene is also beneficial.

10. Be creative. Because you are made in the image of God, you have a creative force within you, and you can't be completely fulfilled unless you express it somehow. Art, music, dance, crafts, photography, writing, baking, and gardening are only a few of the possible outlets for your creativity. Don't worry about whether you're "good enough." If it makes you happy, that's good enough.

11. Get closer to God. By depending on God in your growth, you'll feel his love flowing through you. And you'll just have to accept his opinion that you are a worthwhile and lovable person.

In short, you love yourself by being a friend to yourself. This is far different from being selfish. We are being selfish when we put our own wants and needs ahead of others' and even ahead of God—when we say, "I'm going to do what I want and I don't care how my behavior affects anyone else!" To be selfish is to withhold love. But a healthy degree of self-love actually increases our love for others, as it increases our understanding of them and our capacity for real giving.

You may have been taught a song long ago in Sunday school entitled "Jesus and Others and You Spells Joy." Maybe the teacher wrote it on the blackboard like this:

Jesus	J
Others	O
You	Y

But that diagram makes it look as if you find joy by invariably putting yourself last, by ignoring your own needs. I think false martyrdom wears out joy in a hurry. A better way to diagram it is like this:

Jesus	
	JOY
Others and You	

This way, you aren't below the others—you're one of them. You're equal. You can love your neighbor and be one of your own neighbors. You can consider your own needs as you would consider anyone else's, without putting yourself above others.

Self-love shouldn't be arrogant, proud, self-important, or narcissistic. Self-love isn't selfish, always needing to have its own way. It's just the recognition that "I am a worthy person, created in the image of God—I have potential to do good things." Jesus died for you. If you're worth dying for, you're worth taking care of. Take care of yourself so that you'll be better able to care for others. Jesus worded it this way, "Consider the ravens: They do not sow or reap, they have no storeroom or barn; yet God feeds them. And how much more valuable you are than birds!" (Luke 12:24).

For Further Reflection

On seeing yourself as God sees you, read Genesis 1:27; Psalm 8:3–9; 139:13–16; Proverbs 19:8; Matthew 10:29–31; Romans 8:37–39; Ephesians 3:14–21; 1 John 3:1–3; and Revelation 1:5–6.

18 *Taking Charge of Yourself*

I will exalt you, O Lord, for you lifted me out of the depths and did not let
  my enemies gloat over me.
O Lord my God, I called to you for help and you healed me.

PSALM 30:1–2

Taking care of yourself doesn't mean being selfish or always putting yourself first. It means helping yourself grow and change in a responsible, disciplined way. It means becoming the best you can be and fulfilling the wonderful plan God has for your life. When you overcome the effects on your life of someone else's drinking and/or drug abuse, you are free to become your best possible self.

Are You Addicted to Crisis?

One reason it's difficult to get the focus of your attention off the drinker's life and onto your own is "crisis addiction," or what Toby Rice Drews, in her excellent series *Getting Them Sober*, calls "excited misery."

Life in the family troubled by *chemical dependency* (this term seems to be emerging in scientific circles as the most popular one for alcoholism and drug addiction) often seems to drift from one crisis to the next. (A crisis, for our purposes, is any situation so urgent, traumatic, or upsetting that we feel we must give it our full attention for a time.) A shouting match, an accident, the loss of a job, an incident of abuse—these are just a few of the crises that frequently disrupt the alcohol-troubled family. When a crisis occurs, normal activities screech to a halt as we get all emotionally worked up about the predicament at hand. Even when we still have time to attend to everyday chores, we are so totally involved with the crisis that many things go undone.

Quite naturally, we don't like disruptive things to happen. But I think it is possible to become addicted to that high level of excitement. After a period of years, it can get to seem like a normal way of life. We feel there is no point in making plans, as they are only going to be disrupted anyway. So we drift from one distraction to the next. Then when there isn't a crisis at the moment, life seems mundane and boring. We just can't "get into" raking leaves, doing laundry, or helping Joshua learn long division. And when a new emergency comes along, it is a "relief," on one level, to jump into it.

Crisis addiction makes life easier, in a way, because it "lets us off the hook" when we don't take charge of our own lives. After all, "Who can blame me for being disorganized or having little self-discipline when I always have to drop everything because my alcoholic gets into a scrape or picks a fight with me?" This is an understandable mental habit, but one that has to go.

Eileen was addicted to crisis. Even after her separation from her violent alcoholic husband, she was still always wrapped up in some emergency or another. If it didn't involve her husband, it was her son's behavior problems, office politics at work, or a manipulative friend who was "using" her. Each incident threw her into a tizzy for two or three days. During these times she would neglect her appearance and her home, live on coffee and pastries, and spend endless hours on the phone "hashing it out" with friends. Fortunately, after a couple of years of separation she began to calm down.

Of course, many crises are real and genuinely force us to react in some way, but others don't require any action from us at all because they are just predictable steps in the progression of alcoholism. Some emergencies are real turning points that give us opportunities to change our lives for the better. But the important thing when confronted with a crisis is to calm down and reflect carefully on what we should do. Then we need to act rather than merely react.

Ask yourself these question in any crisis:

- Is this truly important?
- Is it my business to be involved in this?
- Is there anything really constructive I can do?
- Am I taking over responsibilities that belong to others?
- How can I regain some peace and detachment right now?

The Mind Is Still the Key

Always remember that you control what goes on in your mind, and your mind controls what goes on in your life. Your emotions don't control you unless you let them. If you want to let go of crisis addiction and lead a real life, you'll need to gain control of your thought life.

Remember that you can improve your attitudes by concentrating on positive things—on what you are doing or will do today. Take pleasure in your work and recreation, because "the cheerful heart has a continual feast" (Prov. 15:15). When destructive or negative thoughts well up, reject them in the name of Jesus, and substitute something better. I'm not telling you to deny an unpleasant truth; just resist the temptation to dwell on bad things and sink into self-pity. Deal with your emotional injuries, and then put them behind you. Allow old wounds to heal—don't let them control you.

Also, drop the practice of using your drinking loved one as an excuse for your own shortcomings. It is no more valid than if the drinker uses you as his excuse.

Going After Your Goals

Would you find it hard to answer if someone asked you what your goals are for today, this week, and this year? Unfortunately, many people caught up in someone else's problems have no immediate answer to that question. They are too accustomed to living from one crisis to another. They might say, "I just want to get through this day."

Well, just "getting through" isn't enough. But if you are in the "getting through" trap, I understand how and why it happened. It's hard to keep making plans when they are always ruined by someone's unpredictable behavior (or by your own overreaction to that behavior). You need patience and flexibility in carrying out your plans, because there will be setbacks. What you don't need is to give up making plans entirely. You need to plan good things, even great and wonderful things, for yourself and those you care about.

It is important, though, to understand that setting goals does not conflict with living one day at a time. Your goals can be pursued "today only"—one little step at a time. If your goal seems big and overwhelming, break it down into tiny, manageable steps, the first small enough to be completed today. For example, if you dream of becoming a lawyer, you could go to the library *today* and compare college catalogs. If your house is chaotic and you want it organized, you could start *today* by giving away all those old magazines you're never going to read.

Incidentally, an organized home is an excellent goal to pursue. You don't want to be perfectionistic or "crazy clean." But neatness is important, because family members can't really relax or feel comfortable with chaos or extreme clutter. The mess becomes a statement of the family's lack of self-esteem and the "mental junk" that clutters minds. Yes, I *am* speaking from experience. If you have trouble getting organized, I recommend a book that helped me. It is *Side-tracked Home Executives*, by Pam Young and Peggy Jones, published by Warner Books. You need not be a full-time homemaker to profit by their experience.

If something happens today that prevents you from taking even one small step toward your goal, take it tomorrow instead. Just keep going. *Don't ever give up.*

Here are some more examples of long-term goals and the immediate steps you could take toward them:

- "I want to read the whole Bible this year." (I'll read three chapters today.)
- "I want to become a better witness for Christ." (Today I'll say hello to my neighbor and get to know her a little better.)

- "I'd like to spend more quality time with my children." (It's going to be hot tomorrow. Maybe we can have a picnic at the beach.)
- "I need a better-paying job." (I'll talk to my supervisor about learning the skills I need to be promoted.)
- "I want to lose twenty pounds." (I don't need this doughnut.)
- "I'd enjoy taking up art as a hobby again." (I'll find a pencil and spend half an hour sketching something today.)

That gives you an idea of what I mean. There's almost nothing you can't do if you start small, but the important thing is to start *now*. Set one or two goals at a time, not eight or ten. (You know what has happened before when you tried to take on your whole life at once.) Keep charts and lists of what you do in moving toward your goal, so you'll be able to see how you've progressed. Use rewards as motivation—decide on some suitable little gift you'd like and what you have to do to earn it. At the same time, progress toward a goal can make you so happy that it serves as its own reward.

In my case I never thought I could write a whole book. But the Lord kept nudging me with the idea. So I finally said, "Okay, maybe I can write a book, and maybe I can't. But I *can* go to the library, find some material on alcoholism, and take a few notes." After I had a thick stack of note cards, one day I decided I could start to organize them into categories and put together a rough table of contents. This all took years, with setbacks both major and minor.

Starting the actual writing was a hurdle, even though I'd been publishing smaller pieces for a long time. But one day I said, "I think I could start with chapter five. I have a fair idea of what I want to say in it." Now thousands of one-day-at-a-time hours later, the book is coming together. Getting it published is part of the goal. But even if no one else ever reads it, it would still be worthwhile for me to have written it, because I have written it to myself as much as to you, and it has helped me with my own recovery and growth.

What About the Children?

If you are raising one or more children, they are some of the best reasons you have to get control of and take charge of your life. If they are the children of an alcoholic, they have a greater than average chance of becoming alcoholics or codependents themselves. Your best chance of helping them is to help yourself. When you break the cycle of sick relationships within the family, when you are emotionally strong enough to nurture the children, make them feel fully loved, and provide a more normal family environment, they will be stronger and more able to make sane choices as adults.

Children's physical needs—for protection, good food, sleep, cleanliness, decent clothing, shelter, supervision, and medical care—must be met no matter what. Chemical dependency in the family often leads to lapses in care of children even when adults know better. Remember, though, there is nothing you have to do that is more urgent or important than meeting the needs of the children in your life.

A child's emotional needs are as important as the physical needs. Children need direct expressions of your love—they don't just "know" they are loved without being told, hugged, and kissed. They also need spiritual training, consistent discipline, and protection from any kind of abuse. They need to be able to discuss alcoholism and other family problems openly and honestly with at least one parent or other close adult. (Al-Anon offers books and materials that can help you start such a discussion.) Children need to have responsibilities at home, but within reason. Unfortunately, some children of alcoholics are pushed into adult roles prematurely, becoming little homemakers, confidants, and "parents" to their parents.

Don't interfere with the child's relationship with an alcoholic parent any more than necessary. If there is physical or sexual abuse, that to me would be reason enough to separate and take the children to live elsewhere. But if there is no abuse, don't stand in the way when the alcoholic wants to provide good discipline or become involved in the children's lives. Also, there is no need to "protect" the alcoholic from the child by acting as peacemaker in their disagreements or by keeping children out of the way when the drinker "doesn't feel well." The goal here is to have as normal a parent-child relationship as possible.

If the "children" in your life are teens or young adults and have already been damaged to a degree by alcoholism in the home, don't think it's too late to make a difference. Your example is still important to them. If they see you make dramatic improvements in your own quality of life, they will want to know why and how. And then you can tell them.

Self-discipline and Integrity

To overcome a bad habit may be another of your goals in taking charge of your life. You cannot really be in charge if you are enslaved by overeating, pills, smoking, or excessive shopping, television watching, or anything else that seems beyond your control. Your habit may seem to be a comfort because it fills a gap created by the real unmet needs in your life. But wouldn't you rather have your real needs fulfilled?

Remember those wise words of Paul to the Christians in Corinth: "So, if you think you are standing firm, be careful that you don't fall! No temptation has seized you except what is common to man. And God is faithful; he will not let you be tempted beyond what you can bear. But when you are tempted, he will also provide a way out so that you can stand up under it" (1 Cor. 10:12–13). God promises you two things in these verses. First, you are not alone or unique in your temptation, and second, you can resist it.

Two other principles may help you resist what is bad for you. One, you can substitute something better—when tempted, keep busy with something constructive, and think positive thoughts. Two, don't provide for or cater to the desires of your sinful nature in advance. That can mean different things, depending on what your temptation is. If it's food, don't bring home the doughnuts and cookies. If it's spending, cut up your credit cards. If it's pornography, don't enter a store where they sell it. If adultery is a possibility, don't make a lunch date with the person in question.

What about drinking? Although I don't believe an occasional alcoholic drink is a sin, I do think anyone who has lived with alcoholism is wise to be extremely cautious, if not totally abstinent. You could put yourself in danger through various kinds of accidents and through lowered inhibitions if you drink. If you had an alcoholic parent or grandparent, you may be genetically vulnerable to addiction. And even if you are not going to do yourself any harm, you should think about the example you set for others who may be more vulnerable than you are. You have a unique opportunity to show your loved ones that a person can seldom or never drink and still be happy and fulfilled.

Is there anything on your conscience—even something small or something that happened long ago—that keeps you from feeling right about yourself today? Read again the section on guilt in chapter 14. Then make amends to anyone you have hurt, if that's what you need to do. Amends are anything you can do to make things right—an apology, the payment of an old debt, and so on. Sometimes "indirect amends" are the best and most useful kind. An improved attitude toward your loved ones or a reconciliation with someone from whom you have been alienated can be the best policy and can do more good than a "confession" that will only hurt someone.

It takes *self-discipline* to live with a sense of purpose; to take the small, everyday steps that lead to reaching your goals. It takes self-discipline to resist doing what is wrong or is wrong for you. And it takes self-discipline to take care of your rightful responsibilities and take charge of your life rather than be blown around by every wind that comes along. Self-discipline is similar in meaning to "self-control"—one of the fruits of the Spirit (see Gal. 5:16–26). Finally, self-discipline means often doing things that you don't particularly feel like doing at the moment but in the long run will lead to a better way of life.

We have covered a lot of seemingly unrelated topics in this chapter. What makes them all hang together is the concept of "integrity." Integrity is your wholeness or completeness; it is your ability to live according to your own beliefs and be the best possible you that you can be. When you have integrity, you have nothing to hide—your conscience is clear. You can act with confidence rather than react with fear, insecurity, and people-pleasing.

A person with integrity does what is right because it is right, not because of the way other people will or won't react. A person with integrity has values, goals, and faith that are more important than what anyone else thinks. "What you see is what you get" with such a person—all communications are straightforward and honest.

When you have grown into integrity, it won't bother you as much that you can't make your alcoholic happy. You will realize that no one can make another person happy. Each person is responsible for his or her own happiness. You will concern yourself with your own clearly defined responsibilities. You know where the boundaries are between yourself and others. You don't have high walls, but you do have borders. You aren't addicted to crises, because the pursuit of your goals makes your everyday life full and exciting. In short, you are in charge of yourself, and you can be a strong example to the next generation. And with the psalmist you can say to the Lord, "I know that you are pleased with me, for my enemy does not triumph over me. In my integrity you uphold me and set me in your presence forever" (Ps. 41:11–12).

For Further Reflection

On the mind and attitudes, read Romans 8:5–8; 12:2; Ephesians 4:17–24; Philippians 4:4–9; and 1 Peter 1:13–16; 4:7.

On goals, read 2 Corinthians 5:9–10 and Philippians 2:3–4; 3:12–14.

On temptation, read Matthew 5:27–30; 26:41; 6:13; Luke 4:1–13; Romans 6:11–14; 7:14–8:17; Galatians 6:1; and James 1:13–15.

On making amends, read Proverbs 14:9 and Matthew 5:23–26.

On integrity, read 1 Chronicles 29:17; Nehemiah 7:2; and Psalm 25:20–21.

On children, read Psalms 78:1–7; 127:3–5; Proverbs 14:26; 19:18; 22:6, 15; 29:15, 17; Matthew 7:9–12; 18:1–6; 19:13–14; Ephesians 6:1–4; and Colossians 3:20–21.

Part 7   Toward Healthy
          Relationships

———————————————————

19 *Expanding Your Horizons*

He who walks with the wise grows wise, but a companion of fools suffers harm.   PROVERBS 13:20

Until now, we have concentrated on your relationship with your alcoholic loved one and your relationship with yourself. Now let's look at how you relate to the rest of the world.

Overcome Isolation

It is possible, you know, to be around people all day long and never really "connect" with anyone. You can know that you are getting to be too isolated emotionally if

- There is no one with whom you can discuss your problems.
- Your social life is confined to other chemical dependents and their families.
- You can't have "normal" friends, because it's too embarrassing for them to see how you live.
- Old friends have dropped you because they can't take the alcoholic's bizarre behavior.
- You have dropped old friends or involvement in a church or organization you enjoyed because your alcoholic objected to them and gave you a hard time about it.
- You have been talked into moving to some remote place where you don't know anyone.
- You couldn't possibly get into a self-help group or counseling,

because of your drinker's objections or because such things can't even be discussed.
- You feel "no one understands."

As we have said before, the alcoholic wants you isolated so that he or she—and the disease—will come to have total control over you. In the name of tough love, you must learn to recognize this manipulation and refuse to knuckle under to it.

Overcome your fears and taboos. Go to church or your club. See your "normal" friends—alone during the day, if necessary. Discourage any talk about moving away or to the mountains. Get help when you feel you need it. If the drinker keeps you home by being "unable to take care of the children" when you are going out, make other arrangements for them. Above all, don't believe the nonsense that it will "help him or her get sober" when you devote yourself exclusively to the drinker.

Confide with Care

Confide your troubles to God first. After that, most of us have the need for at least one close friend—a person close enough to hear all our troubles and know everything about us. A good confidant helps you overcome self-pity, feel less alone, and relieve the tension that comes from keeping everything inside. In all probability we're talking about one such friend, or a very few at the most. Don't make a bid for sympathy by confiding in practically everyone you know.

What kind of person is the ideal confidant? He or she

- Is a mature Christian with a good spiritual perspective.
- Has some understanding of chemical dependency.
- Is a good listener who won't interrupt you, misinterpret what you say, or quickly give unasked-for advice.
- Is not related to you or the alcoholic. Relatives seldom have the necessary detachment; they take sides.
- Can keep a confidence. (Watch out for friends who gossip. If they do it to everyone else, they'll do it to you.)

- Doesn't overload you with sympathy but helps you see that you have choices.
- Is in no danger of starting to "rescue" you—take over your decisions or do things for you that you should do for yourself.

Remember the wise words of the wisdom writer, "A righteous man is cautious in friendship" (Prov. 12:26).

Relatively Speaking

Even without chemical dependency, extended families involve complicated relationships. Relatives tend to become too emotionally involved with one another's problems. There is a tendency to feel they must come up with "answers" for you. It's wonderful to have them around when you need practical help, but do all you can to discourage them from becoming overinvolved or rescuing either you or the drinker.

If there are other alcoholics, drug abusers, and codependents in the family, these problems are greatly magnified. Unhealthy, overinvolved family relationships will likely be so common that family members don't understand what a normal relationship is. Then, when you get into a recovery program and begin to regain control over your own life and responsibilities, they won't understand you at all.

If family members are always getting you down or spoiling the good effects of your recovery, you may need to stay away from them for a time. If that makes them angry, you'll have to accept their anger as normal. Just say to yourself, "Of course, they don't understand. They're just like I used to be." Don't push the truth too hard; they will see it when the time is right, just as you did.

Keep in mind, too, that it is always possible that some relative or close friend will take over your role in "rescuing" your drinker after you give it up. He or she may lend him money, drive her home, bail him out, lie for her, take over his work for him. In all probability this will make you feel angry and frustrated now that you know how bad this is for an alcoholic. In addition it may trigger your irrational guilt, too, and cause you to say, "That's *my* job." But that makes no sense at all; that's why we call it irrational.

What is even more upsetting to you is that you feel you are being considered a bad person for giving up your rescuing role. But, let's face it, there is nothing you can do about this situation without making yourself look even worse to the other "rescuer." Just wait it out, and hope the do-gooder wakes up to what is happening. At least your time is now free for more useful activities.

You Can't Rescue the World

In all probability you are a very nurturing and loving person, and that's a wonderful attribute. The world needs more like you. But it can be overdone.

It is possible you have what I call the mother-of-the-world syndrome. Are your friends always the ones who need you rather than the ones you need? Do you jump into other people's arguments in the peacemaker role? Do you sometimes get into trouble by giving unwanted advice? Do you do things for others that they could and should be doing for themselves? Watch out for excesses in your nurturing, because they can spill over into unhealthy rescuing.

If you are doing over 50 percent of the "work" in a relationship over a long period of time, you are probably acting out the role of rescuer. What do you get out of it? And while it is true this role makes you feel indispensable and saintly, it is liable to destroy the relationship sooner or later because of the resentment that can so easily surface. You may feel rejected if your advice isn't followed. And the other person may become resentful because of the feeling you are interfering.

Every person needs to examine his or her "rescuing" motives. Are you bent on being a "rescue" person because of your great love for humanity? Or do you really like having a certain amount of power and control over another person? If you're thinking the other person "can't make it without me," that's your ego talking.

Many codependents end up in the "helping professions": nursing, social work, and counseling. Even here, you can avoid rescuing.

Though the professional-client relationship is inherently unequal, there are certain proper boundaries and limitations to it. You can observe those. Also, you should be encouraging your patients and clients to become less dependent, not more.

It is also possible that your alcoholic's drinking buddies may appeal to you as an outlet for your "mothering" energies. This is a unique sort of friendship. Sometimes a cozy group of loyal drinking friends exists together in a fantasy world of their own creation. They believe one another's denial as if it were the gospel and see the world as conspiring against them.

Though such people can be both pathetic and appealing, avoid the temptation to "save" them. If you let them, they will consume all your time. Instead, work on your own life and problems. Spend time with people who are good for you. And if you are sometimes thrown together with the drinking buddies' codependent family members, share with them what you are learning, but be gentle if they aren't ready for it.

Getting Help

It is important to understand that alcoholism is too much for a person to deal with alone. Reading a book like this may not be enough. Human beings are meant to work together in partnership and in dependence on God. In this way, we come up with better answers and learn more about love and how it works. There are several different kinds of outside help available to you. Be selective, and utilize those particular aids that meet your needs at a given moment. In doing so, you'll come across secular influences and ideas that may conflict with your beliefs. That's okay. Just run everything through your mental and spiritual "filters," and take only what you can use effectively.

Al-Anon Family Groups, an offshoot of Alcoholics Anonymous, is a self-help organization for family members and close friends who need help in dealing with someone else's drinking. At first some people go to meetings to learn "how to make him stop drinking." But that isn't what the group is about. The emphasis is on helping yourself by changing your response to the drinking. Its philosophy is similar to what you've already been reading in this book. If you go, the members won't let you focus on complaining about the drinker. Instead they will help you examine yourself to see how you can improve your reactions.

Some well-meaning Christians object to Al-Anon because it isn't specifically Christian. I have never felt there is anything in it that is incompatible with my faith. Al-Anon encourages you to depend on a Higher Power, so all you have to do is define your Higher Power as Jesus Christ. It is true that some people define their Higher Power differently. But AA and Al-Anon need to have this kind of openness if they are to help a variety of people with many different beliefs and backgrounds. However, many members acquire a hunger for deeper spiritual truths through this process and move on to a deeper understanding of Christian faith.

You may ask, Why do I need Al-Anon when I have my church? Well, it could be that many of your church leaders know little about chemical dependency. That is often the case. So why not let church and Al-Anon work together in your life to teach you how to apply the wisdom of God's Word to this particular situation?

You can find Al-Anon meetings by calling the number listed in most big-city telephone books, or through your local police agency, church office, or Chamber of Commerce. If one group doesn't suit you, try another.

You can also seek help through individual counseling. Most likely you can find a therapist or counselor through your church, your medical doctor, or a community health center. In selecting a counselor, it is important that he or she be knowledgeable about alcoholism. And, of course, it is a plus if he or she is a Christian. Such relationships are highly individual, so if you don't mesh with one counselor, ask to be referred to another.

Be prepared for therapy to be hard work, as you face unpleasant feelings and decide what changes need to be made in your life. It is likely, too, that therapy will help you find more strength than you thought you had. Be prepared, too, for your alcoholic to feel threatened by your therapy or your participation in Al-Anon or any other self-help group. But if that happens, just keep on doing what's best for you. Don't let your strings be pulled by somebody else.

In addition, if there is need, there are shelters for battered women and children, support groups for those who have suffered abuse, and programs for displaced homemakers who need to return to the job market. And there is legal aid available if you are considering a legal separation or need a court order to keep a violent person away from you.

At the same time don't overlook the help that can be yours through the church. Pastoral counseling can be a big help. Though some pastors have little experience with alcohol or drug abuse, others are quite knowledgeable. When I went through a brief separation years ago, I got good advice from my pastor. I also received practical help in setting up an apartment from church people I had thought would be judgmental and reject me!

Help for the Alcoholic

I would also encourage you to check out the programs for alcoholics that are available in your area—AA, inpatient and outpatient hospital programs, counselors, therapy groups, and so on. Also check out the services that your health insurance will cover. In this way you'll be well prepared when your alcoholic is ready to accept help.

Treatment can save lives. But over the long term much depends on the alcoholic's own motivation. Treatment can't make a person get well who doesn't want to. Sometimes, however, a drinker may enter treatment just to get a spouse or employer off his or her back but then will get the proper motivation to undertake what is necessary for recovery. It is important not to pin all your hopes on any program: if your loved one gets into treatment, be happy, keep praying, and keep working on your own recovery so that you'll be prepared for whatever happens.

Again, the wisdom writer gives us good advice, "Perfume and incense bring joy to the heart, and the pleasantness of one's friend springs from his earnest counsel" (Prov. 27:9).

For Further Reflection

On friendship and help, read Psalm 18; Proverbs 12:26; 16:28; 17:17; 18:24; 20:18; 27:6; Romans 8:26–39; and 1 Corinthians 12:12–28.

20 *The Bottom Line*

God is our refuge and strength, an ever-present help in trouble.

I'd like to close this book by restating its main ideas, chapter by chapter:

1. Drinking is a firmly entrenched social custom, but alcohol addiction is a serious social problem from which we all suffer.
2. Abusers of alcohol (and other harmful drugs) harm themselves physically, financially, mentally, emotionally, and spiritually. Others around them suffer too.
3. It isn't a contradiction to say that drunkenness is a sin *and* alcoholism is a disease. Some people may have a genetic predisposition to alcohol addiction.
4. By the time you have to ask whether someone has a drinking problem, most likely the answer is yes. When someone's drinking disturbs you, it's more important to deal with your problem than to find the "right" term for it.
5. You can't stop someone else from drinking, but you can improve your own life by changing your reactions to the drinking and related behavior.
6. Alcoholics and their affected loved ones (codependents) tend to deny the problem and pretend it doesn't exist, but we must give up denial before we can get anywhere.
7. There is a right way and a wrong way to confront the drinker about the effects of his or her behavior on *you*. It isn't judgmental to point out that there is a problem.

8. Alcoholism breeds fear, but God provides practical ways to overcome your fears.

9. Faith is the answer to fear, but faith in anyone or anything but God is misplaced.

10. Faith that is real will be put to work, but we must do some thinking and praying about which actions are really good works. Love that is tough love is motivated by what is best in the long run for the one you love.

11. Detachment, or letting go of emotional overinvolvement and obsession with the drinker, leads to serenity and peace.

12. We each have responsibility for our own actions, not for others'. We must stop protecting alcoholics from the consequences of their own behavior.

13. To be angry is not wrong in itself. It is better to recognize anger and deal with it constructively, and to accept others realistically, than to swallow our anger and hold grudges.

14. Like anger, spiritual poisons like self-pity, envy, self-righteousness, lack of forgiveness, inappropriate guilt, and depression must be faced and replaced with more positive feelings. It's good to take some time out to refuel when "burned out."

15. Even when the alcoholic dumps his or her self-loathing on you through projection, most domestic arguments can be avoided or minimized through wise management on your part.

16. Verbal and emotional abuse, intimidation, and physical abuse are serious problems that call for firm action. It is not an act of love to submit to mutual destruction. There is a right way for a married Christian to separate if necessary.

17. To love yourself is to recognize the high value God puts on you as a person. Self-esteem is not selfishness, and you can rebuild yours if it has been damaged.

18. Rather than "go with the flow" of alcohol-related crises, we must take charge of our lives by setting goals and working toward them. Integrity is being true to yourself and your own beliefs.

19. If alcoholism has isolated you emotionally, you can reach out

to others in a healthy way, get the help you need, and give to others without "rescuing" them from their own responsibilities.

These ideas are the result of my own search for a better life over a period of ten years or more. That's all they are: ideas. I'm not an "expert," a doctor, a social worker, or a member of the clergy. I'm an ordinary Christian person, just trying to grow and become all the Lord wants me to be. The ideas in this book have helped me to become a much stronger and more "together" person over the years, I believe, perhaps stronger than I would be if I'd never had the relationship that troubled me and caused me to look for answers in the first place.

I hope some of what I have learned helps you to be stronger and happier too. If not all my ideas suit you, then of course you'll "take the best and leave the rest," as they say in Al-Anon. I have pictured "you," the reader, as a friend and an equal, sitting across my kitchen table and discussing these things with me.

God bless you in your search for *your* truth and for a faith you can live by. Always "walk in the light." Go in peace.